KU-251-648

DANIEL BELL

MALCOLM WATERS

Professor of Sociology
University of Tasmania

UNIVERSITY OF WOLVERHAMPTON
LIBRARY

2022004 CLASS

CONTROL
0415105773

DATE
25 JUL 1996 SITE

WITHDRAWN

London and New York

First published 1996
by Routledge
11 New Fetter Lane, London EC4P 4EE

Simultaneously published in the USA and Canada
by Routledge
29 West 35th Street, New York, NY 10001

© 1996 Malcolm Waters

Phototypeset in Times by Intype, London
Printed and bound in Great Britain by
Mackays of Chatham PLC, Chatham, Kent

All rights reserved. No part of this book may be reprinted or
reproduced or utilized in any form or by any electronic,
mechanical, or other means, now known or hereafter
invented, including photocopying and recording, or in any
information storage or retrieval system, without permission in
writing from the publishers.

British Library Cataloguing in Publication Data
A catalogue record for this book is available from the British Library

Library of Congress Cataloging in Publication Data
A catalogue record for this book has been requested

ISBN 0–415–10577–3 (hbk)
ISBN 0–415–10578–1 (pbk)

Contents

Figures

Preface

The idea that the *Key Sociologists* series should include a volume on Daniel Bell came originally from Chris Rojek, formerly Senior Editor in Sociology at Routledge. When he suggested it to me on a sunny Friday afternoon at an end-of-term departmental celebration here in Hobart it seemed an instantly appropriate and appealing project and it has remained so long after the conviviality of the occasion has been forgotten. Bell is an attractive and important figure and, although I could claim no particular scholarly expertise in his work at the time, I realized that it had had an important influence on my own efforts, as well as those of others, to theorize social change. Bell's work is a central element in the sociological canon and, like it or not, it infuses the discipline, often guiding the direction of sociological thought and always challenging orthodoxies, whether they be functionalist, Marxist or empiricist.

I owe a huge debt of gratitude to Dan Bell himself. When I wrote to him, without the benefit of an introduction or intermediary, asking if he would allow me to interview him he agreed without hesitation. He kindly received me into his home, making himself available for a couple of solid four-hour sessions which must have been a source of physical strain. He was as feisty and combative as his writings reveal him to be, but he was always co-operative and tolerant of critical questioning. Even though the strains of jet lag affected me towards the end of those sessions I shall especially remember the vigorous and unrelenting intellectual curiosity that he continued to display right through the lunches that Pearl Bell had so generously prepared. Perhaps the excellent Australian Semillon that he served helped to stimulate the flow of intellectual juices.

My other debts are also considerable. Mari Shullaw and Ann Gee of Routledge took over the project when Chris Rojek moved on. My trip to interview Daniel Bell was partly funded by a School of Humanities and Social Sciences Research Grant from the University of Tasmania. Robert White proof-read the manuscript and identified a number of classical allusions in Bell's work that have found their way into the notes. Christina Parnell patiently transcribed interview tapes that did not always offer the highest quality of sound. As ever, Judith Homeshaw and Penny and Tom have been with me all the way.

Malcolm Waters
Hobart, Tasmania

1

Return of a Prodigal Son

In the early 1970s Kadushin (1974) conducted a major research exercise to seek to establish the membership of the American intellectual elite. Using a sampling methodology that was only somewhat flawed he defined (public) intellectuals as people who contributed to a set of widely circulating magazines and journals but who were not themselves full-time journalists. He then surveyed this group, following a reputational methodology, to try to discover who was most influential among them, who constituted the elite. By counting votes he came up with a list of 70 names. He divided these 70 into three ranks according to 'natural breaks' in the distribution: the top ten, the next ten, and the rest. By dint of alphabetization, Daniel Bell's name can be found first among the top ten (1974: 30–1).[1] He sits alongside such other key public figures as Noam Chomsky, John Kenneth Galbraith, Norman Mailer, Susan Sontag and Edmund Wilson. There is no other sociologist in the top ten, although Hannah Arendt and David Riesman are in the top twenty and Edgar Z. Friedenberg, George Lichtheim, Nathan Glazer, Seymour Martin Lipset, Robert K. Merton, Robert Nisbet and Franz Schurmann can be found lower down alongside W. H. Auden, Marshall McLuhan and Barrington Moore. The list includes neither of the leading theoretical sociologists, Alfred Schütz and Talcott Parsons, nor does it include either the leading empirical sociologists, Otis Dudley Duncan, Erving Goffman and Paul F. Lazarsfeld or the philosophers of social science, Carl Hempel and Ernest Nagel. Put simply, Kadushin's research confirms the fair estimate that Daniel Bell is probably the most famous sociologist of the post-war generation[2] and, for that reason alone, a series on 'key sociologists' would be incomplete without a volume describing his work.[3]

Bell did not, however, become a famous sociologist by being a popularizer, like his nemesis, Alvin Toffler, that purveyor of what Bell calls 'future schlock'. Rather, his influence derives from his capacity to take big ideas, that may or may not be of his own origination, and to have the courage and tenacity to run with them. While they may not be universally acceptable, all of them are pieces of good sociology because they have centred wide-ranging and long-standing academic debates. He is responsible for three big ideas that any professional sociologist will recognise: the end of ideology, the post-industrial society and the cultural contradictions of capitalism.

Bell first mounted his argument about the end of ideology in 1955 (EI;[4] also see Chapter 4). It suggests that party politics is entering a phase in which it is no longer governed by the extre-mist ideologies of the left and right and in which the political parties that are the major contenders for power are in broad agreement about the need for a mixed economy, a welfare state and liberal democracy. The post-industrial-society thesis was first mobilized about ten years later (COPIS; also see Chapter 6). It proposes that socio-economic structures are entering a major historical phase-shift out of manufacturing goods and towards the production of services. This shift is accompanied by an intellec-tualization of technology, the rise of a scientific knowledge class and a renewed communalism in politics. Bell floated his third big idea, that capitalist societies are riven by threatening and disrup-tive contradictions at the cultural level, as a sequel to the post-industrial-society thesis (CCC; also see Chapter 7). It argues that capitalism originated in a coherent relationship between an economy that demanded work discipline and a Protestant culture based on frugality and abstemiousness. As capitalism has developed, these 'realms' have been driven apart by an increasing emphasis on consumption. The main contradiction of capitalism lies between the continuing stress on discipline and hierarchy in the economy and an emphasis on the gratification of the self in the culture. For Bell this disjunction and its several subsidiary contradictions will eventually result in a decomposition of culture unless a fundamental reversal takes place.

These ideas have always been controversial and are fully accepted by almost no-one other than Bell himself. However, they have remained continuously on offer in the market place for sociological ideas since they were first formulated. It has now become impossible to address the prospects for long-term social transformation or to consider the turns being taken by modern culture without addressing Bell. We can begin this retrospective on his work with a brief examination of the biography that stimulates and directs it.

BIOGRAPHY[5]

Bell was born 1919 in the Lower East Side of New York City, in what used to be called the 'garment district'. Most of his family had chain-migrated from the Bialystok area that lies between Poland and Russia. The patriarch was his paternal grandfather who sold coal in winter and ice in summer from a horse-drawn cart. The family name was Bolotsky but this was probably an invention only a few generations old, constructed to avoid military service. His father died when Bell was eight months old and he lived, along with his mother and siblings, with other extended kin, usually maternal sisters, until about 1927. Because his mother was employed full time as a pattern-maker, he was often placed in a Hebrew day orphanage according to the demands of work on his mother's time. By the age of 11 Bell had a new legal guardian, his paternal uncle Samuel Bolotsky. Samuel was a dentist and upwardly mobile and the name Bolotsky did not fit such a career. So a group of cousins got together to choose new names – some became Ballin, some Ballot and some Bell. Notwithstanding these developments, Bell experienced the full gamut of poor, immigrant Jewish experience: Yiddish as the first language, Hebrew school, ethnic street gangs, petty crime, racketeering and the public poverty of waterfront shacks.

By his own supposition, these experiences of poverty predisposed Bell to become a socialist. When he was 13 he joined the Young People's Socialist League, one of a number of socialist groups that lived in an uneasy relationship with the Jewish garment-workers' unions. He joined after reading Upton Sinclair's *The Jungle*, declaring to his *melamed* (teacher) that he had found the truth and no longer believed in God. An enduring picture of Bell is that at that tender age he spent long hours in the Ottendorfer branch of the New York Public Library reading not only socialism but sociology. By the age of 15 he was taking courses in dialectical materialism at the Rand School of Social Science. He was tempted by communism in both its Trotskyite and Stalinist varieties but he was persuaded by Rudolf Rocker, an old Anarchist, to read Berkman's pamphlet 'The Kronstadt Rebellion'. Reading about Trotsky and Zinoviev's brutal decision to put down by force the naval mutiny at Kronstadt in 1921 persuaded Bell to remain a democratic socialist. At the City College of New York (CCNY) where he joined a socialist reading group called 'Alcove No. 1' Bell was regarded as something of an oddity. The other members, who included Meyer Lasky, Irving Kristol, Nathan Glazer and Irving Howe, were mainly Trotskyites and many were later to convert to become the core of the neo-conservative movement. In the fashion of a Talmudic scholar Bell knew his Marx verbatim but he remained opposed to violent revolution and committed to a mixed economy.

In retrospect, Bell interpreted his choice in terms of Weber's famous distinction between the 'ethics of responsibility' and the 'ethics of ultimate ends' (1981). Like Weber he believes that simultaneous adherence is impossible because the former can involve a loss of principle while the latter sanctions abhorrent means. Like Weber, Bell opted for the ethics of responsibility because it provided the best answer to the question: 'Given the existing conflict, how can I solve it with the least internal and external damage for all concerned?' (1981: 537)

When Bell went to CCNY in 1935 he majored in classics rather than sociology. He chose to do so on the advice of a brilliant young communist instructor named Moses Finkelstein[6] who suggested that ancient history was the best preparation for sociology because one could there examine entire and coherent cultures. After he graduated in 1938 Bell spent a year in graduate school at Columbia University but without any apparent result. He left, for reasons unexplained, and spent most of the next 20 years of his life working as a journalist.[7] Most of the war years were spent at the *New Leader*, a vehicle mainly used by social-democratic supporters of the union movement, first as a staff writer and then as managing editor. From 1948–58 he was a staff writer and then Labor Editor at *Fortune*, the voice of American big business. In these roles he learned about the realities of political struggle and he also learned how to produce large volumes of written material quickly. He estimates that he wrote 426 articles in the 20 years after 1948 (WP: xviii n). Bell never lost this journalistic facility, even after entering academic life on a permanent basis. Indeed, the high point of his journalistic career might have been in 1965 when he founded *The Public Interest* with Irving Kristol as a forum for the rehearsal of great public debates.

Bell's academic career began as early as 1945 when he accepted a three-year appointment teaching social science at the University of Chicago. Later, during the Fortune years, he moonlighted as an adjunct lecturer in sociology at Columbia (1952–6). However, he moved out of journalism permanently in 1958 as an Associate Professor in the same university. He recalls his conversation on the occasion with the proprietor of *Fortune*, Henry Luce:

> When I left *Fortune* in 1958 Mr. Luce was puzzled at my decision and asked for the reasons, with the thought that he might be able to match a rival offer. There are, I told Mr. Luce, four good reasons for going back to academe – June, July, August and September. Mr. Luce thought that more money might compensate for time, but I decided otherwise. I have never regretted that decision. [WP: xix n][8]

He received his Ph.D. from Columbia in 1960 for a compilation of his published work and was promoted to full Professor in 1962. He moved to Harvard in 1969 and was appointed to his prestigious endowed chair as Henry Ford II Professor of Social Sciences in that university in 1980.

Bell never shrunk from public life to the closeted comforts of the ivory tower. Most of his public service was devoted to insisting on a sociological contribution to planning for the future at the national level. He was seriatim: a member of the President's Commission on Technology, Automation and Economic Progress 1964–6 and co-chair of its Panel on Special Indicators; chair of the *Commission on the Year 2000* that he founded under the aegis of The American Academy of Arts and Sciences, 1964–74; American representative on the OECD's Inter-futures Project, 1976–9; a member of the President's Commission on a National

Agenda for the 1980s and chair of its Panel on Energy and Resources; and a member of the National Research Council Board on Telecommunications and Computers.

In the later years of his career, Bell has been the recipient of numerous honours, prizes and visiting lectureships. The most prestigious of these include: Guggenheim Fellowships in 1972 and 1983; the Hobhouse memorial lecture at the University of London, 1977; Vice-President of the American Academy of Arts and Sciences, 1972–5; the Fels Lecture at the University of Pennsylvania, 1986; the Suhrkamp Lecture at Goethe University, Frankfurt, 1987; the Pitt Professorship in American Institutions and a Fellowship of King's College, Cambridge, 1987–8; the American Academy of Arts and Sciences Talcott Parsons Prize for the Social Sciences, 1992; an American Sociological Association Award for a distinguished career of lifetime scholarship, 1992; and no less than nine honorary doctorates.

Bell retired from his professorship in 1990 and, rather than return to the distracting pulsations of New York, chose to remain within the leafy serenity of Cambridge, Massachusetts. He lives just across the street from the American Academy of Arts and Sciences to which he devoted much of his energy and at which he continues to hold the position of Scholar-in-Residence. He is still active:

> [I]n recent years I have returned to journalism as a means of supplementing my retirement income, and in the last years I have done a considerable number of articles, most of these on economic and political questions. I write a monthly article for Shukan Diamond, a Japanese weekly on business affairs, and that article is now 'syndicated' by me and appears in Korea, Indonesia, Mexico, Italy and Spain. Occasionally, these appear in *Dissent* an American quarterly, such as a long one on the break-up of American capitalism. [Bell to Waters 30/8/93]

VALUE-COMMITMENTS

It is clear from his writing that Bell experiences all the torture of the contradiction between being a deep believer in the capacity of religion to provide meaning and simultaneously of not being a practising member of any religion. The key prodigal act was the declaration of atheism and the embracement of socialism that he made when he was thirteen.[9] While he has long-since returned from socialism, the return to religious practice has been much more difficult.

> I am Jewish [but] I am not a Jew by faith in the funda-
> mentalist sense; I'm not a believer in the narrow sense.
> I am a Jew by fate in terms of who we are. And that, it
> seems to me, has always been true, that Judaism has
> never been religion. Judaism is defined as being a people.
> [Simons 1988: 68]

Yet the promise of a cultural tradition that can stably provide meaning and morality remains tantalizing because the ties of ancestry remain: 'I am bound, in the faith of my fathers, to the thread, for the cord of culture – and religion – is memory' (WP: 354). Even a secularized ethnic Jewishness holds particular tensions for the intellectual – to embrace cosmopolitanism is to deracinate oneself, to make ethnicity central closes oneself off from the main debate. Bell is, therefore, in an important sense, a homeless wanderer.

> I have found no 'final' place, for I have no final
> answers. I was born in *galut* and I accept – now gladly,
> though once in pain – the double burden and the double
> pleasure of my self-consciousness, the outward life of an
> American and the inward secret of the Jew. I walk with
> this sign as a frontlet between my eyes, and it is as visible
> to some secret others as their sign is to me. [WP: 322]

This tension is, according to Bell's friend and mentor, Irving Howe, directly reflected in his sociological output.

> [W]e thought we should know everything. . . . Meyer
> [Schapiro], I would say, is the ultimate example of the
> whole idea of range and scope. On a more modest level
> somebody like Danny Bell lives by the same notion.
> Behind this is a very profoundly Jewish impulse: namely,
> you've got to beat the goyim at their own game. So you
> have to dazzle them a little. [Howe 1982: 284]

The return from socialism was accomplished much more easily, although it has been the topic of much secondary speculation, often from Trotskyites who cannot make sense of the reversion (see e.g. Brick 1986; Leibowitz 1985). It happened in 1947 and, in retrospect, Bell describes it thus:

You see, a young man who's very ambitious, such as I was, wants to write a book. In '44–'45 I began a book and had a contract with John Day for a book called the Monopoly State. . . . I began sitting daily in the New York Public Library, in that famous room 315, and reading and reading, and suddenly I thought: all this is silly. I only know this second-hand; I know this by imputation: I'm using some mechanical categories; I'm making comments on them, and it's all silly. I suddenly realized I was educated in a vulgar Marxist framework, if you want to put it that way, making imputations about corporate behavior and I never really knew what was going on. And suddenly I felt that all this was silly. I had a manuscript that was about 300 to 400 pages and I looked at it and I said to myself: this is really nonsense. [Leibowitz 1985: 65]

It is possible that Trotskyites and others make too much of Bell's reconstruction and too little of the reconstruction of some others from the CCNY study groups more committed to communism, such as Howe, Lasky, Glazer and, *in extremis*, Kristol. Although Bell read Marx he was never a Communist, unless a Menshevik, so that the reversion was more like a deviation towards the centre than a *volte face*. Importantly, it coincided with several significant biographical developments, not least the move from *New Leader* and *Common Sense* to *Fortune*. Bell's personal rejection of ideology was linked to an academic interest in its societal rejection. His first monograph (MS; see Chapter 4), published in 1952, examined the failure of socialism in the USA and he also worked on the collapse of ideological extremism on the right (RR). The culmination, of course, was the end-of-ideology thesis that was originally produced for a conference of the *Congress for Cultural Freedom*, a London-based, anti-communist intellectual group that, probably unknown to Bell, received some of its income from the CIA (Wald 1987: 351).[10]

The milieu that brings together the issues of religion and political ideology is the 'New York Intellectual Circle':

These New York Jewish Intellectuals came together as a self-conscious group, knowing each other, discussing ideas they held in common, differing widely and sometimes savagely, and yet having that sense of kinship which made each of them aware that they were part of a distinctive sociohistorical phenomenon'. [WP: 130]

They had a common Jewish immigrant experience, they often spent their early years as socialists if not communists, and they were educationally mobile, often through CCNY and Columbia. In its maturity, the tone of the circle was distinctly illiberal, refusing to denounce McCarthyism or the American military engagement in Vietnam, opposing affirmative action for blacks and women, standing radically opposed to student protest, and endorsing unquestioning American support for the state of Israel. They were highly integrated – Kadushin finds that over 50 per cent of the American intellectual elite lived in NYC and that about half of that elite was Jewish, although he does not specify the exact overlap (1974: 22–3)[11]. More importantly, most of the key intellectual journals were located there.

There is little doubt that Bell was a key figure in the circle, partly by virtue of his contacts with the inner group and partly because of his editorship of some of the more influential periodicals. However, he has always rejected the label 'neo-conservative' that Michael Harrington invented for many of its members even though such authors as Steinfels (1979) always include Bell in the category.[12] In support of Bell's claim it must be admitted that he has always criticized the bureaucratic yoke to which American labour finds itself harnessed and he condemned as shameful the carpet bombing of North Vietnam and the invasion of Cambodia ordered by President Nixon in the 1970s. On the other hand, he was deeply critical of the student protests of that decade on the grounds that they were selfish threats to intellectual traditions and academic communities. Because they were more balanced, his views were sufficiently out of tune with the rest of the circle that he eventually resigned his editorship of *The Public Interest*.[13] Nevertheless, hc continues to define himself as a New York Intellectual even though the meaning of that term is now, in his view, somewhat attenuated: 'I suppose that the "New York Intellectuals" are more relevant as a style of work than anything else' (Bell to Waters 30/8/93).

If Bell's moral and political commitments appear to be complex he would not himself disagree. Indeed, he is committed to the notion that one can hold seemingly contradictory value-commitments in relation to the different realms of society (CCC: xi-xv). At the peak of his career he could confidently state: 'I am a socialist in economics, a liberal in politics, and a conservative in culture' (CCC: xi) However, his economic socialism might be thought to be a very personal creed.

> For me, socialism is not statism, or the collective owner-
> ship of the means of production [but] that *in this realm*,
> the community takes precedence over the individual in
> the values that legitimate economic policy. . . . This means
> a set of priorities that ensures work for those who seek
> it, a degree of adequate security against the hazards of
> the market, and adequate access to medical care and
> protection against the ravages of disease and illness.
> [CCC: xii-xiii; original italics]

Under this view, each family ought to receive at least the minimum income required to meet its needs. Wealth, he believes,
should not be a basis for privilege in access to such services as
health care and education.

Political liberality implies two principles: first, that the individual rather than class, race, gender or ethnicity should be the
primary political actor; and second, that a distinction must be
maintained between the private and the public spheres. In the
public sphere, Bell insists, there must be equality of opportunity
but not necessarily equality of outcome. He therefore supports
wage differentials on the functionalist principle that they can
mobilize talent and effort and he would be opposed to affirmative
action. In other words, he is committed to the principle of merit
in reward distribution and to minimum state action in the spheres
of morals and economics.

Possibly the most controversial of Bell's value-positions is the
one he takes in relation to culture: 'I am a conservative in culture
because I respect tradition; I believe in reasoned judgments of
good and bad about the qualities of a work of art; and I regard
as necessary the principle of authority in the judging of the value
of experience and art and education' (CCC: xv). He rejects any
democratization of culture in which all individual experience is
regarded as worthily meaningful and in which all cultures are
of equal value. He therefore stands opposed to such bodies of
knowledge as 'cultural studies' that directly make such claims. It
is also clear, although not explicit unless in RGE (see Chapter
5), that Bell regards elite-bourgeois-white-male-Western culture,
what he calls the Western cultural tradition, to be richer and
more developed and thus superior to any other. There is little by
way of political correctness or post-colonial sensitivity or postmodern sensibility here.

Bell insists that these positions while apparently contradictory are in fact consistent.

> The triune positions I hold do have a consistency in that they unite a belief in the inclusion of all people into a common citizenship through that economic minimum which allows for self-respect, the principle of individual achievement of social position on the basis of merit, and the continuity of the past and present, in order to shape the future, as the necessary condition for a civilized order. [CCC: xv]

Bell's value-positions are indeed mutually consistent but possibly only because his definition of them is itself at variance with normal understandings. But an enquiry into that issue must be saved for the conclusion of this book.

SOCIOLOGY

Bell's interest in sociology originated in his youthful experience, just as his socialism did.

> I had grown up in the slums of New York. My mother had worked in a garment factory as long as I could remember; my father had died when I was an infant. All around me I saw the 'Hoovervilles,' the tin shacks near the docks of the East River where the unemployed lived in makeshift houses and rummaged through the garbage scows for food. Late at night I would go with a gang of other boys to the wholesale vegetable markets on the West Side, to swipe potatoes or to pick up bruised tomatoes in the street to bring home, or to eat around the small fires we would make in the street with the broken boxes from the markets. I wanted to know, simply, why this had to be. It was inevitable that I should become a sociologist. [1981: 532]

Well before attending CCNY he was browsing the sociology stacks in the New York Public Library. He remembers reading Robert Hunter's *Poverty* and Spencer's *Principles of Sociology*. Of course, the main early reading was Marx, so that Bell, surprisingly to some, remains to this day one of the most knowledgeable, if not the most conventional of Marxist scholars in the discipline.

At Chicago Bell experienced his first large encounter with

academic sociologists. There he team-taught a common course in social science with 'an extraordinary group of young thinkers' (WP: xvii) including David Riesman, Edward Shils, Milton Singer, Barrington Moore, Morris Janowitz and Philip Rieff. These scholars represent a tradition now, save Bell, largely lost in American sociology, of theorizing long-term societal transformations and the problems they pose for social organization, that is, of doing substantive, general theory that lies between the sterilities of grand theory and empiricism. The subsequent move to Columbia can be seen as part of the return of the prodigal to Jewish roots. In fact, though, the influences there were mixed. Columbia indeed housed the sociological wing of the 'New York intellectuals', Philip Selznick, Seymour Martin Lipset, Nathan Glazer, Alvin Gouldner and Bernard Rosenberg, most of whom were sometime graduate students of Merton and Lazarsfeld. But, for Bell, 'the primary influences were Robert McIver and the Horkheimer group, as well as a neglected figure, Alexander von Schelting, who had written a book on Max Weber's *Wissenschaftslehre*, and gave a reading course in Weber's *Wirtschaft und Geselschaft* that I took' (Bell to Waters 30/8/93). It is possible to recognize the influence of Horkheimer and Adorno particularly in a sociology of culture that theorizes contemporary culture as the product of the drive for consumption. However, Bell denies this: 'If there are sources it would not be Horkheimer, but more likely Matthew Arnold and Trilling' (Bell to Waters 10/9/93). More importantly, all of these influences introduced Bell to the Weberian tradition but it was Weber in the proper guise of historical sociologist rather than Weber as a Parsonsian action theorist.

By contrast with the experiences at Chicago and Columbia, Harvard sociology appears to have influenced Bell very little. He seldom mentions any colleague sociologist from that university. This may be because when he moved there he was invading the territory of an academic opponent. The Harvard department is most frequently associated with the structural-functionalist theorist, Talcott Parsons who worked there for some 40 years. Bell's major books, COPIS and CCC, are debates with the holistic theories proposed by both Marxism and functionalism.

> A Marxist or Functionalist views society as some kind of historical period or closed system, integrated through the mode of production or dominant value system, and believes that all other, superstructural or peripheral,

realms are determined by or predominantly influenced by this principle of 'totality' or 'integration.' Against these holistic views, I have argued that society is better understood as being composed of diverse realms, each obedient to a different 'axial' principle which becomes the regulative or normative standard of action in each realm.' [WP: xx; some punctuation deleted]

If one were to seek to locate Bell in relation to the classical triumvirate of founding ancestors one would say that he is closest to Weber, most opposed to Marx and most neutral in relation to Durkheim, notwithstanding labelling as a Durkheimian (e.g. Archer 1990; O'Neill 1988). Otherwise, he is perhaps most influenced by the sociologists of his generation such as Aron, Shils, Riesman and Dahrendorf, but he is unimpressed by structural-functionalism, symbolic interactionism and abstracted empiricism. He has read such contemporary British sociologists as Goldthorpe, Mann and Runciman, as well as the work of his niece's husband, Stephen Lukes, but not what is often known as 'French theory': 'It may startle you, but I have never read Lyotard and that literature. What I have seen I regard as shallow' (Bell to Waters 10/9/93). However, what really impresses when one reads Bell is not his knowledge of sociological writings in particular but the breadth of his familiarity with the canon of the Western intellectual tradition. He is influenced at least as much by Aristotle, Rousseau, Schumpeter, Nietzsche, Veblen, Saint-Simon and Kant as well as members of the New York circle, chief amongst whom he would probably count Howe, Kristol, Trilling, Glazer and Sidney Hook. If he did intend to 'dazzle the goyim', he succeeded in at least one instance.

Bell is a relentless publisher. By his own count he has written or edited 14 or so books and a best guess would suggest about 200 articles of a scholarly nature. The articles tend not to be published in sociology journals. He has published once in the *British Journal of Sociology* (the Hobhouse memorial lecture) but only reviews in the *American Journal of Sociology* and the *American Sociological Review*. His preferred outlets are non-refereed, general intellectual journals often associated with the New York circle, with other Jewish interests or with learned societies, including *The Public Interest, Commentary, The Partisan Review, New Leader, Dissent, Daedalus*, and *The American Scholar*. His books often reprint his articles and the articles often reprint prefaces written for books. The three most important, influential and best-selling books are the ones that express the three 'big ideas', *The End of Ideology* (1960), *The Coming of Post-industrial Society: A Venture in Social Forecasting* (1973), and *The Cultural Contradictions of Capitalism* (1976). Each of these is a collection of articles previously published, rather than a monograph.

STYLE AND METHODS

Bell writes in a fluid, limpid prose style. The text is peppered with references to the canon and with non-English words and phrases that are only occasionally annoying. The style is resolutely conservative and, for this reason, sexist, being littered with references to 'man' and 'men' while women are scarcely mentioned. Bell is an essayist, the master of the pithy argument, full of punch and challenge. The essay, he says, is his natural *métier*:

> In my first two decades as a writer, I found that my natural length was a 3,000- to 5,000-word essay, something I could do in a week. In the later decades, it has been the 30,000- to 40,000-word essay, a length that could be completed during the summer. [WP: xix]

Along with this change in length has come a change in style so that his essays, he says, have become more theoretical, philosophical and methodological in view of the need to offer a convincing alternative to holism in sociological theory.

However, this essayistic style is not without its unsatisfactory aspects. Essays, especially if they are published in friendly non-refereed journals, are not always subjected to highest levels of rigourous social-scientific criticism. They do not, therefore, always meet conventional standards of precision and logic. Bell's essays are therefore mixtures of good social science, anecdote, personal philosophy and exegesis. Moreover, because they are written as ends in themselves they are often mutually inconsistent. This is not always problematic because every scholar's *oeuvre* evolves, but in Bell's case it presents special difficulties because his major books are collections of unreconstructed essays. One might wish for the production of coherent monographs on the big ideas to match those that Bell produced so expertly on his smaller ones (MS; SS; RGE).

Bell is committed to theoretical generalization; not the formal sort as written by Parsons or Habermas, but generalization of a kind that focuses on historical substance. He enjoys telling a story that illustrates the point, as on the occasion cited here, during the Hobhouse memorial lecture on religion.

> In 1938–9, I was a first-year graduate student in sociology at Columbia University. One of the visiting professors was T. H. Marshall from the London School of Economics, and he offered a course on 'Social Evolution,' based principally on the work of Hobhouse. I enrolled in this course. In due time, Professor Marshall invited me to discuss the term paper that I would write for the course. 'What do you specialize in?' he asked. Without irony, and without the wit to realize it, I replied: 'I specialize in generalizations.' He blinked in mild astonishment, bit on his pipe, but did not pursue the theme. He asked what topic I had chosen for my paper, and I replied, 'The moral bond in Greece.' 'Which aspects of it do you intend to cover?' he asked, and I replied, 'All of them.' He sucked on his pipe, and said only, 'Oh.'
>
> I am pleased to recall that I received an *A* for that paper. But I regret to say that those early, and by now incurable bad habits have remained. When asked recently by my friend David Martin which aspects of religion I would cover in this talk, I said, 'All of them.' He blushed quickly, but said only, 'Oh.' [WP: 325]

Because he is attacking the fortresses of holistic sociology Bell feels the need to employ an explicit methodological armoury in pursuit of generalizations. To examine any period of history, Bell argues, one needs to set up a 'social framework'. A social framework is a conceptual schema that specifies the institutional structures that constrain the lives of individuals (for further detail see Chapter 8). Another word that Bell uses for such a schema is a *prism*, an observational device that can refract and split a society into components that can be examined independently. However, what one sees depends on the particular prism one selects. A prism is therefore a 'synthetic construct', an ahistorical 'ideal type' that treats a phenomenon as a closed system (CCC: xvi). Each schema or prism 'rests on' an *axial principle* and has an *axial structure* (COPIS: 9–10). However, the definition of what is meant by an axial principle or axial structure is, as one might expect from an essayist, interpretive rather than analytic: 'The idea of axial principles and axial structures is an effort to . . . specify, within a conceptual schema, the *organizing* frame around which the other institutions are draped, or the *energizing* principle that is a primary logic for all the others' (COPIS: 10). It is probably reasonable to specify an axial principle as the orientation or end-state of any social arena and an axial structure as the social arrangements by which that end-state is accomplished. On this view, the formulation is analogous with 'function' and 'structure' in structural-functionalism. Bell would vehemently disagree with this interpretation, but if one examines, for example, his view that efficiency is the axial principle of the modern economy and bureaucracy is the axial structure, the parallel becomes apparent.

In his mature work in COPIS and CCC Bell typically follows a particular procedure. He first sets out the 'essential lineaments' of a social formation in a conceptual prism comprising axial principles and structures. He then makes a generalization, e.g. 'the USA is becoming a post-industrial society' or 'the realms of culture and social structure are becoming increasingly disjunctive'. He then confirms the accuracy of the generalization by either or both of two means. One is to consider the empirical complexity of the phenomenon through 'the prism of history'. The second is to extract secular trends from statistical social indicators. However, this description should not leave the impression that Bell's procedures are either formal or direct. The work gives more of the flavour of a *grand tour d'horizon* than of a rigourously formalized analysis.

This book addresses Bell's work in smallish, relatively digestible portions. Each chapter is sufficiently self-contained to be read alone as a discreet introduction to a part of Bell's work. Three of the chapters focus on the big ideas, and three others on work, education and technology. The book begins with a review of the three realms argument within which Bell's work can be seen to have been organized. In general, all of these chapters concentrate on Bell's specifically sociological contributions rather than the more journalistic and politically *engagé* pieces that he wrote prior to 1952.

2

The Three Realms

When Daniel Bell was first appointed to a full-time academic post at Columbia in 1969 American sociology was mainly divided between two hostile camps. On one side were ranged the big battalions of grand theory, sociologists who sought to mobilize highly abstracted, formalized and generalized batteries of interconnected concepts to unify sociological thought about society. The leading grand theorist was Talcott Parsons of Harvard University who had sought not only to unify sociological theory but to integrate within his paradigm of structural-functionalism the theoretical cores of anthropology and psychology as well. Parsons' 'general theory of action' was a theory not only of the social system but also of culture and personality. Indeed, he was later to extend his theory to encompass the biological organism, the physical environment of action and even the supernatural realm of ultimate values. The opposition to grand theory consisted of the mobile, fact-mongering and rationalistic forces of positivistic empiricism that sought to reject not only grand theory but any theory at all, particularly any theory constructed in terms of value-relevance. In line with the strategies set out by Paul F. Lazarsfeld and George A. Lundberg, and armoured by the philosophical legitimations established by Carl G. Hempel and Ernest Nagel, such figures as Hubert M. Blalock and Otis Dudley Duncan could harry and undermine grand theory by hurling at it a limitless arsenal of correlation co-efficients, significance tests and null hypotheses, all accomplished within an anxiety-free technicism. As Alexander (1982) shows, grand theory succumbed to the vandals of positivism and American sociology entered a barbaric period.

This is not to say that there was no alternative. Theoretically weak and empirically inexact, symbolic interactionism had managed to limp on in the sociological imagination, largely by dint of the iconoclastic efforts of such figures as Howard S. Becker and Erving Goffman; and Alfred Schütz had shepherded the influence of European phenomenology into American sociology, although in its new host it mutated into the bizarre and only briefly influential form of ethnomethodology. Bell rejected all of these possibilities. As we have seen, he wanted to be a theorist and a generalizer but he found that he could not accept a holistic vision of society that would deny the possibility of contradictory processes and interests and of divergent historical trends. Acutely tuned to shifts in moods and ideas, he found Parsonsian thought to be inflexible and incommodious in relation to contemporary developments and he has seldom allowed himself to be impressed by sociological positivism.

Holism is an orientation in which all aspects of society are contained within a single system, in which these elements are evenly and continuously connected and in which the system is driven through time by a unitary dynamic or logic. Bell locates the origins of sociological holism in Hegel (CCC: 8–9) who specified that each period of history is unified by a particular *Zeitgeist* or spiritual character. Within each period, Hellenistic, Roman or Christian, every aspect of culture is determined by its connection to its religious core so that each has a particular 'style' that ramifies through politics, art, philosophy, etc. The most sociologically influential purveyor of the Hegelian tradition is Marx, although for him historical periodicity is determined not by *Zeitgeisten* but by specific modes of material production. Here, ancient, feudal and capitalist modes of production ramify throughout society, so that, in the capitalist case for example, we find a formally democratized polity and a commodified culture integrated with a production system based on private property and contractual wage-labour.

As the previous chapter indicates, Bell rejected Marxist holism as a sociological paradigm when he rejected communism as a personal political commitment. In more intellectual terms Bell rejects Marx because he subscribes to numerous fundamental internal inconsistencies (WP: 107–8), because his predictions of where and how socialist revolutions would occur are demonstrably false (CCC: 10) and because of overwhelming substantive evidence of disintegration, disjunction and divergence between the various elements of societies. For Bell, capitalist societies do not necessarily have similar cultures or polities and indeed, in any given society, the culture or polity may work against the maintenance of the capitalist mode of production.

Parsons' grand theory is not of precisely similar order to that of Hegel and Marx. For him a society is a system in which four functions must be fulfilled if it is to survive (adaptation to the environment, goal specification, internal integration and latent provision for the maintenance of social patterns across time). These functions are performed by the specialized institutions of society (respectively, economic, political, communal and cultural). The driving logic is the effort by the system to maintain equilibrium between the various specialized functional performances. Bell applauds the attempt as an honourable failure, 'one of the intellectual feats of that generation' (SS: 43), but regards it as a failure none the less. The reason is that a general theory such as that of Parsons that seeks to integrate all aspects of action has to be couched at a very high level of abstraction. Such an endeavour can be attempted in principle in economics, for example, because there the rates of exchange between system components can be quantified. But in sociology this is not possible because the media of exchange specified (power, influence, commitment, etc.) cannot be quantified. It is therefore impossible to establish what the determinate relations are between the components of the social system (SS: 42–3) and Parsons can therefore only offer us a logically ordered set of formal categories. In criticizing Parsons, Bell voices doubts as to whether any unified theory of society is possible.

A DISUNIFIED THEORY

The alternative scheme proposed by Bell is as general as that of Parsons or Marx but is differentiated into realms or spheres, each of which has its own independent logic of development through time. At the most general level the human condition transpires in three realms or orders: nature, technology and society (WP: 3–33). Human experience involves encounters with, transformations of and knowledge of each. We address them in turn.

Nature is 'a realm outside of man whose designs are reworked by men' (WP: 8). It has two components: the *Umwelt*, the geographical environment, the world of organic and inorganic objects that is open to human intervention; and *physis*, the pattern of natural relationships that can be accessed only by analysis. Humans transform nature by imposing a temporal structure upon it: the *Umwelt* is sequentially re-ordered across history; while *physis* is temporalized by the successive, historically located, 'scientific' paradigms by which people understand it. The earliest interpretations were mythical in character, giving human capacities to non-human objects, and focusing on the *Umwelt*. They were succeeded in turn by the abstracted measuring devices and concepts of science that emphasized *physis*. Subsequently, people returned their attentions to the *Umwelt* as they actively intervened in nature by invention, architecture, engineering, experiment and production. In the process, the human relationship to nature was transformed from that of victim to that of dominator. Bell identifies the prophets of this transformation of human perspectives on nature as Bacon, the essayist who conceptualized science in terms of the progressive accumulation of knowledge by experiment, and Marx, who established that human needs could only be met if human groups organized in order to transform nature.

'Technology is the instrumental ordering of human experience within a logic of efficient means, and the direction of nature to use its powers for material gain' (WP: 20). *Technology* changes along five dimensions (WP: 20–1):

- function increasingly dictates the shape of an object;
- natural energy is increasingly replaced by inanimate sources of energy;
- replicas of objects can be multiply reproduced at decreasing marginal cost;
- possibilities expand both for communication and for machine control of human activities; and
- algorithms (symbolized rules of decision) progressively displace human judgment.

Technology clearly impacts on nature in so far as it opens up

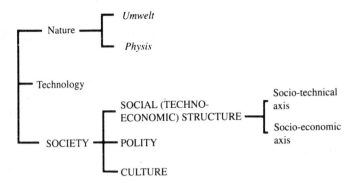

Figure 1 The scheme of three realms

possibilities for the transformation of the *Umwelt*, but it also has profound implications for society, creating consumption-based mass societies, elaborately differentiated occupational systems and syncretized cultures.

Against Durkheim's version of society as *sui generis*, Bell is a convinced social constructionist for whom *society* is 'a set of social arrangements, created by men, to regulate normatively the exchange of wants and satisfactions' (WP: 29; italics deleted). In elaborating this idea Bell reveals himself to be a genuine contractualist:

> Society is a moral order, defined by consciousness and purpose, and justified by its ability to satisfy men's needs, material and transcendental. Society is a design that, as men become more and more conscious of its consequences and effects, is subject to reordering and rearrangement in the effort to solve its quandaries. It is a social contract, made not in the past but in the present, in which the constructed rules are obeyed if they seem fair and just. [WP: 29][1]

As people transform society it moves in the direction of increasing internal complexity and external interdependence.

However, the tripartite division into nature, technology and society is not the most important instance in Bell's sociology. He also subdivides society into three areas: the social or techno-economic structure (TES), the polity and culture (see Figure 1). There is some inconsistency in terminology: in WP (3–33), the three realms are nature, technology and society while the three *dimensions* of society are *social structure*, polity and culture (WP: 31); but in CCC (10), the *techno-economic structure*, polity and culture are distinct realms. Further, in WP the latter trinity is said to be a feature of all societies, but in CCC Bell is agnostic on whether the scheme can be applied generally and reserves it only for modern society (CCC: 10). However, apart from the single essay in WP, Bell generally uses the word 'realms' for the societal trinity and this is the usage that will be employed throughout this book. We can take the second confusion to mean that the three realms are universal aspects of all societies but become separate and autonomous only in modern society.

The epistemological status of the three societal realms is also unclear. They are distinguished from one another by their differing axial principles and different rhythms of historical change. Bell insists, therefore, that they are analytic constructs that can be distinguished from one another only in that scholastic fashion – they are a prism or ideal type (CCC: xvi) through which one can view society. Yet in insisting on their distinctiveness and mutual autonomy he reveals a realist tendency:

> They are not congruent with one another and have different rhythms of change; they follow different norms which legitimate different, and even contrasting types of behavior. It is the differences between these realms which are responsible for the various contradictions within society. [CCC: 10]

Analytic constructs do not, one must insist, follow norms or exhibit behaviour or engage in acts of legitimation because they are structured only by logic rather being constrained by substance. Only substantive systems or concrete units can have these characteristics. Indeed the general tenor of Bell's claims about contemporary social change confirms that he is not engaged in a formal elaboration of analytic constructs at all but rather in a substantive theory of societal transformation that is actually much to be preferred. That said, we can now examine the three realms in some detail.

The *techno-economic structure* is the realm of economic life, the arena of social arrangements for the production and distribution of goods and services. Such activities imply applications of technology to instrumental ends and result in a stratified occupational system. The axial principle of the modern TES is functional rationality. It consistently drives towards minimizing cost and optimizing output and is therefore regulated by the process that Bell calls *economizing*. So we assess the development of the TES in terms of its level of efficiency, productivity and productiveness. Indeed, change proceeds along the path of substituting technological processes and social arrangements that are more productive and efficient for those that are less so. Contra Weber, who locates the development of bureaucracy in the emergence of the modern state, Bell argues that bureaucracy is the axial structure of the TES. The more that technological functions become specialized the greater is the need to co-ordinate these functions and therefore the more elaborate and hierarchical become the organizational arrangements that human beings put in place to accomplish such co-ordination. The lifeworlds of the TES are, in a terminology that might be traced to Lukács (1968), 'reified' worlds in which the individual is subordinated to roles specified in organizational charts. They are also authoritarian worlds that subordinate individual ends to the goals of the organization orchestrated by a technocratic management that recognizes the validity only of the functional and the instrumental (CCC: 11; WP: 31).

The *polity* is the set of social arrangements that frames a conception of justice and then regulates social conflict within that framework. Justice is elaborated within a set of traditions or a constitution. Regulation is accomplished by applications of power, that is, by the legitimate use of force and, in many societies, by the rule of law. It is therefore a system of societal authority involving the distribution of legitimate power in society. In a modern society, the axial principle specifies that power is legitimized by reference to the consent of the governed: 'The polity is *mimesis* in which the forms are known and men choose those appropriate to their times' (WP: 31). Moreover, this axial principle is egalitarian in so far as it specifies that each person must have a more or less equal voice in providing this consent. Because equality of political participation gives expression to the material and cultural aspirations of all members of society, it extends into other areas of social life via the institution of citizenship that implies equality of access to legal, social and cultural entitlements. The axial structure is a system of representation that allows general consent to be expressed through organized arrangements, that is, political parties, lobby groups and social movements, that can funnel claims to the centre. Bell admits that much decision-making in the polity is technocratic in character but insists that political outcomes are the consequence of bargaining and dealing between interest groups or by authoritative resolution at the highest level of the judicial system (CCC: 11–12).

Bell's version of *culture* is much narrower than the conventional sociological or anthropological definitions that specify it as the overall pattern or shape of life in a society. While recognizing that culture includes the cognitive symbolizations of science and philosophy (CCC: 12n) as well as the character structure of individuals (WP: 31), he restricts his interest in culture to the arena of expressive symbolism: 'efforts, in painting, poetry, and fiction, or within the religious forms of litany, liturgy and ritual, which seek to explore and express the meanings of human existence in imaginative form' (CCC: 12). These expressive symbolizations must always address what Bell regards as the universal and irreducible fundamentals of human existence, the nature and meaning of death, tragedy, heroism, loyalty, redemption, love, sacrifice and spirituality (CCC: 12; WP: 31). The axial principle of modern culture is self-expression and self-realization, that is, the value of cultural objects must be assessed against the subjective sentiments and judgments of those who produce and consume them, and not against objective standards (CCC: xvii). The axial structures of modern culture are arrangements for the production and reproduction of meanings and artefacts.

Bell has systematized the three-realms argument within two typologies or grids (Figures 2 and 3). Figure 2 provides what he calls his general schema of society, a kind of meta-grammar or structure that constitutes a universal system for the analysis of societies, identifying all the aspects in which sociologists might be interested. Variation within each of the characteristics specified will determine the characteristic shape of a society. Figure 3 shows that characteristic shape for modern society, revealing how the specific axial principles that apply to each of the three realms ramify through into its detailed practices. The relationship between the two figures is analogous to the structuralist-Marxist specification of structure and formation.

DISJUNCTION BETWEEN AND WITHIN REALMS

Bell is quite explicit in asserting that 'there are not simple determinate relations among the three realms' (CCC: 12). This is because the direction and the pattern, what he often calls the rhythm, of change in each of them is fundamentally different. In

Realm	Techno-economic (social) structure	Polity	Culture
Axial principle	Use of tools to increase resources	Stipulation of legitimate power	Existential meanings
Axial structure	Organization of production	Institutions of rulership	Aesthetic and religious authorities
Central value-orientation	Relationship to nature	Justice	Transcendence
Relationship of individual to social order	Individual as instrumental means	Jural standing	Meaning of self defined by the ultimate
Basic processes	Differentiation	Definition of actors and arenas	Tradition and syncretism
Structural problematics	Disruption of custom Material scarcity	Nature of rights and obligations	Reconciliation of 'release' and 'restraint'
Pattern of change	Lineal	Alternating	Recursive

Figure 2 The general schema of society
Source: Adapted from grid supplied by Daniel Bell

Realm	Techno-economic (social) structure	Polity	Culture
Axial principle	Functional rationality	Equality	Self-realization
Axial structure	Bureaucracy	Representation	Reproduction of meanings and artefacts
Central value-orientation	Material growth	Consent of the governed	Novelty and originality
Relationship of individual to social order	Role segmentation	Participatory	Sovereignty of the whole person
Basic processes	Specialization and substitution	Bargaining and legal reconciliation	Disruption of genres by syncretism
Structural problematics	Reification	Entitlements, meritocracy and centralization	Postmodernist anti-nomianism

Figure 3 The disjunctive realms of modern society
Source: Adapted from grid supplied by Daniel Bell

the TES change is linear or progressive, involving an upward curve in production and efficiency. This is because economizing provides a clear set of rules about innovation and substitution. More efficient and productive machines, techniques and organizations displace less efficient and unproductive ones. So the social aspects of the TES follow a Durkheimian path: 'The enlargement of a social sphere leads to greater interaction, and this interaction in turn leads to specialization, complementary relations and structural differentiation' – this is especially the case in economic enterprises (CCC: 13).

There is no such rule in the polity, where the pattern of change consists in alternation between opposing configurations. People can alternate between the efficiencies of oligarchy and the equalities of democracy, between the expertise of elitism and homogenization of mass society, or between the unifying tendencies of centralization and the localism of confederate systems (WP: xx, 31). The polity is the least theorized of the three realms. For example, Bell does not make clear what he means by the phrase, 'Definition of actors and arenas' in Figure 2. However, it is clear that the choices between these alternatives are the outcome of interaction between political interest groups. At no point does Bell suggest that the outcome is determined by conflict between such groups or by the direct subordination of some groups by others. Rather, in modern polities (which presumably and with difficulty must include the fascist and state-socialist examples) the choices are made as the consequence of negotiation and bargaining. Each political formation is, in effect, a deal or trade-off between interests. In so far as the 'people' represent themselves as an interest group, the outcomes will be representative and democratic.

By contrast, cultural change is recursive. Culture repeatedly returns to the central questions of human existence (death, love, heroism, etc.). In so doing, culture, unlike the TES or the polity, never rejects its past. As Bell nicely puts it, 'Boulez does not replace Bach' (CCC: 13), but merely enlarges the musical repertoire, adding his style to the warehouse and increasing future possibilities for expressive symbolization. However, Boulez addresses the same expressive questions as did Bach so that it is only the form of the answer that changes. While retaining its past, culture can follow one of two paths in developing upon it. It can follow the additive, developmental and incremental path of tradition, building on well-established genres but not stepping outside them. Alternatively, it can engage in indiscriminate mixing and borrowing from several, diverse cultural traditions. This syncretism can apply both to art, where avant-gardes normally involve an unpredictable and unlikely jumbling of styles, and to religion, 'the mingling of strange Gods' (CCC: 13). Because of its axial principle of self-realization, modern culture is radically syncretistic, allowing to each individual the freedom to produce and consume within any style that it encounters. Indeed, individuals are continually encouraged to explore new styles, find new experiences, and choose for themselves. Tradition offers no burden of orthodoxy and each cultural opinion has the same value as any other – modern culture is anti-nomian. Tradition, then, occurs in what Bell somewhat tautologically calls 'stable societies' (WP: xx), while syncretism occurs as the consequence of cultural contact, where segmented societies or parochial cultures break down (CCC: 13).

Because the rhythm of change is different in each realm, each follows its own path through time and thus each has its own separate history. In certain periods of time the particular formations apparent in each of the realms will be synchronized and there will be an accidental unity between them. Bell identifies twelfth-century Europe and the 'apogee' of bourgeois society in the last third of the nineteenth century as examples of such periods (WP: xx). However, at other times, perhaps at most other times, the realms will be disjunctive, that is, their normative specifications will contradict one another at the level of experience. Disjunction between the realms is a structural source of tension in society and is therefore the fulcrum of change. In contradistinction to holistic theories of society, Bell's theoretical approach proposes, then, not only that disjunction of the realms is a normal condition of society but also that it is the central feature of contemporary society in particular.

Bell can now identify a series of disjunctive tensions between the realms as follows (CCC: 14):

- the TES specifies bureaucratic norms of hierarchy and authority but the polity stresses equal participation and consent;
- the TES specifies the virtues of efficiency and thrift, while the culture emphasizes profligacy; and
- the TES segments roles and specializes tasks, while the culture emphasizes gratification of the whole self.

These disjunctions lead to further contradictions *within* each of the realms, for example (WP: xi-xii):

- the TES seeks to encourage an ethical commitment to work so that workers will produce, but also an ethical commitment to hedonism, so that they will consume;
- the culture celebrates the collapse of traditional bourgeois arts and the victory of avant-gardes while simultaneously recognizing the collapse of modernism in the face of massification;
- the polity seeks to provide material entitlements to an increasing range of non-productive claimants while seeking to protect citizens' rights to the benefits of their own productive labour; and
- the culture prescribes secularization yet fears disenchantment.

The future consists of attempts to resolve these contradictions. But, in Bell, structure begets action so that contradiction stimulates social conflicts expressed in the ideological terms of alienation, loss of community, depersonalization and the diremption of authority. However, if these problems are the consequence of the structural disjunctions between the realms then we cannot solve them but must simply wait until the three cogs of history intermesh once again.

THE HISTORY OF MODERN SOCIETY

If the three realms are the analytic prism through which Bell observes society, then history is the substantive prism. Speaking broadly, Bell's history of modern society is a narrative on the tensions and 'crossovers' (interpenetrating influences) between TES and culture, with the polity acting as an arbitrating referee between them. The overall picture is one of initial unification of the realms, followed by divergence, disjunction, internal contradiction and ultimately the self-destruction of culture.

The initial pattern of unification is contained in the formation known as 'bourgeois society'. It involves a conjunction between individual entrepreneurship and personal economic responsibility in the TES, liberal resistance to the constraints of an enlarged and active state in the polity, and an emphasis on expressing the self, rather than a set of issues prescribed by tradition, in culture: 'When capitalism arose as an economic system, it had a tenuous unity: an ethos (individualism), a political philosophy (liberalism), a culture (a bourgeois conception of utility and realism), and a character structure (respectability, delayed gratification, and the like)' (COPIS: xxi). However, a radical hiatus rapidly developed between the TES and culture. At first it involved a contradiction between the disciplinary constraints of work and the quest for a personal sense of the sublime and for emotional excitement in cultural expression. The more the ethic of work disappeared and the more that human labour became subjected to an authoritarian hierarchy, the more cultural tradition was eroded. Social legitimation, as Bell puts it, passed from the sphere of religion to modernism itself, to the cultivation of the individual personality. The economy responded to this demand, mass producing cultural artefacts and images. Modernism turned into a restless search for titillation and novelty, a 'rule of fad and fashion: of multiples for the *culturati*, hedonism for the middle classes, pornotopia for the masses. And in the very nature of fashion, it has trivialized the culture' (CCC: xxvii). The following paragraphs trace the specific developments in the three realms that bring about this disintegration.

Techno-economic structure

Drawing on Marx's distinction between *forces of production* and *social relations of production*, Bell makes a critical distinction between two dimensions of the TES: technology and property relations (COPIS: x-xi). The history of the TES transpires independently in each of these dimensions. Technology passes through three principal phases: a pre-industrial phase based on craft manufacturing and the extraction of primary products; an industrial phase based on the application of machines and inanimate sources of power to the fabrication of goods; and a post-industrial phase in which technology becomes automated and informatic and human labour is increasingly devoted to the processing of information (see Chapter 6). Property relations provide four possibilities that Bell appears to derive directly from Marx, although unlike in Marx they are not entirely arranged in an evolutionary sequence: ancient/Asiatic slavery in which human beings can themselves become property; feudalism in which land is inalienably owned by noble families; capitalism in which property is alienable and is owned by private individuals and families; and socialism (or collectivism) in which property is owned by the state on behalf of all the members of society. Variations between modern TESs can be specified in relation to these dimensions

Property relations

	Capitalist	Collective
Industrial	USA	China
Pre-industrial	Haiti	Cuba

Figure 4 Dimensions of modern techno-economic structure
Source: based on COPIS: x–xii

see Figure 4). In this paradigm, then, we can inspect another expression of Bell's commitment to the view that the material base does not determine or unify society. Although societies may converge on industrialism or post-industrialism this does not mean that historically they become alike in all respects. Modern Western society is a unique configuration that requires historical elaboration.

For Bell, the origins of industrial capitalism can be located in aspects of character structure identified by Weber and Sombart. Weber emphasizes Protestant asceticism, the thrifty abstemiousness that leads to the prudential bourgeois emphasis on methodical calculation. By contrast, in a wider conceptualization of capitalism that extends to mercantilism, Sombart's emphasis lies on acquisitiveness, a trait found equally in Catholic contexts. Acquisitiveness drives the bourgeois in the direction of risk-taking, innovation and exploration. The intersection of asceticism with acquisitiveness is, for Bell, the source of both instrumental rationality and of restraint on sumptuary behaviour. But the restraints of religion were progressively attenuated and bourgeois capitalism became boundless, restless and energetic, colonizing and remaking the natural world in its own image. Nevertheless, the energies of the bourgeoisie were strictly confined to the economic realm, to accumulating capital so the individual self was realized through great techno-economic works.

This Protestant ethic was undermined by internal developments. It had restrained not only bourgeois profligacy but also any proletarian quest for freedom from the disciplines of work and production. As a consequence, systems of production have become more rigid than they once were. Bell views industrial enterprises as bureaucratic dinosaurs weighed down by regulative processes that prevent their adaptation to rapidly changing markets and by defensive unions that fix tasks and rewards. Flexibility is further constrained by the development of a state that seeks to restrict the impact of economic enterprises in reconstructing nature, especially in the environmental field. Capitalist enterprises had remade themselves, not only to constrain the aspirations to individual freedom of their workers but to expand production in the direction of massification. While workers were expected to be restrained while on the job, capitalist expansionism also required that they should be unrestrained consumers in their domestic contexts. The masses had to be puritans at work and hedonists at home, or as Bell puts it: 'a corporation finds its people being straight by day and swingers by night' (CCC: xxv). So during the middle 50 years of the twentieth century capitalism was rejigged to produce 'the life styles paraded by the culture' (CCC: xxv) in the forms of consumption goods produced to meet wants rather than needs and also in the form of mass-mediated images.

Within this transition, the distribution of economic power changed markedly. Bell often describes early capitalism as 'family capitalism' under which private property was the source of individual power (see Chapter 3). Society was run by an elite group of ruling families. The mass expansion of capitalism was marked by a separation of ownership and control so that property became corporate rather than private. In a formulation that might owe something to Burnham, access to managerial positions has become based on technical skill rather than ownership and is therefore non-heritable. Contra Mills, of whom Bell was, on Horowitz's description, a 'pugnacious' and 'ungenerous' opponent (WP: xiv; see Bell on Mills in EI: 47–74; WP: 138–43), this becomes the source of an attenuation of managerial power. Management loses the legitimations that derive from a confident self-conception of a natural right to rule. Indeed, Bell is quite convinced that, in contemporary society, power has all but passed from the TES to the state because of the incapacity of the economic order to manage the systemic problems of society (CCC: xxviii). It is to the history of that realm that we can now turn.

Polity

In modern society the development of the polity is shaped as much by 'crossovers' from the economy as by its own internal logic. A liberal, non-interventionist state could no longer survive. In transforming itself to a mass bureaucratized scale the TES initiated society-wide problems that could not be resolved within the TES itself. Bell (CCC: 23–4) enunciates five such problems:

- the capacity of the TES to grow continuously and its efforts to stimulate sumptuary behaviour led to a public sense that citizens were entitled to a rising standard of living;
- the realization that there were insufficient resources to satisfy all the diverse and contradictory wants and values that the society generates – liberty and equality, education and income, defence and social security;
- the generation of 'spillover' effects, especially environmental degradation and pollution;
- the emergence of endemic inflation as the consequence of a simultaneous commitment to economic growth and full employment; and
- the failure of the 'disaggregated' market to make the crucial economic decisions that might have resolved these issues.

As a consequence, during the middle of the twentieth century Western states started to organize their economies. The first step in this development occurred in the 1930s when states intervened under the imperative need to rescue economies from the market failures of the Great Depression, and it received a further boost under conditions of total commitment to the World War of the 1940s. But in the post-war period a consensus emerged on two issues: the importance of fiscal policy in maintaining a balanced pattern of demand, wage-costs and investment; and the need for the state to underwrite scientific research and education because of both its military and its economic applications (CCC: 255). In the middle of the century then, Bell can characterize political action by the phrase 'state-directed economy', but in the last quarter of the century the state has generalized its intervention beyond fiscal steering so that we now have 'state-managed societies'. This is a response to the revolution of rising entitlements and the diversity of demands in which the organization by the state of health, education, welfare and social services has become the norm. The state has become committed not only to being a welfare state but to redressing economic and social inequalities (CCC: 226).

In contemporary society, certainly where it is post-industrial, the state rather than the economy has become the centre for distributional struggles. Bell is still just about willing to call them 'class struggles', although only in sneer quotes and only because of their parallels with genuine class struggle (CCC: 24–5). More accurately, they are attempts to influence the distribution of that 50 per cent of national income controlled by Western governments by status-claimants operating as pressure groups. Thus, the main political practice is 'fiscal sociology', an attempt by government to theorize the standing of these status-claimants and to allocate taxation revenue to them.

Bell briefly considers possibilities for a totally corporatized state in the USA (CCC: 25–6), but he believes that it is an unlikely development. Managers have a culturally entrenched resentment against governmental regulation, and radicals of both the left and right view any advance in governmental power with deep suspicion. More importantly, such a state would run up against the liberal values of civil society, Hobbesian values that Bell himself apparently shares:

> [T]he state management that will emerge will be a cumbersome, bureaucratic monstrosity, wrenched in all directions by the clamor for subsidies and entitlements by various corporate and communal groups, yet gorging itself on increased governmental appropriations to become a Leviathan in its own right. [CCC: 25]

In a generalization that stretches across both the Atlantic and the Pacific, Bell argues for an inhospitable reception for corporatism because Western societies lack both a willingness to sacrifice individual welfare against common welfare and a philosophical framework that can legitimize distributional priorities.[2]

Culture

Although modern culture is the main topic of Chapter 7 of this book, we can here consider an outline of Bell's view of its development (CCC: 16–30, 37–57). As will be becoming clear, for Bell, individualism is central to modernity. Individualism implies that the person is the most important unit of society, against the family or the state, and that individuals each have a natural right freely to express themselves and to evaluate the morality of their own behaviour or the behaviour of others on the basis of a reflexive inspection of the conscience. For Bell, the cultural equivalent of the bourgeois entrepreneur is the autonomous artist, freed from ecclesiastical and aristocratic patronage, and seeking to have artistic products evaluated as a commodity in the market. The juxtaposition of individual self-expression with the vagaries of the market is both the fulcrum and the problematic of modern artistic production.

However, the autonomisms of the bourgeois and the artist rapidly became incommensurable. Bell describes the familiar, nineteenth-century image of: 'a coterie of artists, engaged in difficult experimental work to which the smug middle-class audience responded with scorn and outrage' (CCC: 38) that became the dominant, if romanticized, motif of modern art (including literature, film, sculpture, etc.). It could not succeed unless practised in the enclave of a garret or a *Quartier Latin* that would allow it to be avant-garde and without being in tension with its societal host. Against bourgeois values, the Romantics and Impressionists claimed the superiority of the individual mind and its perceptions, and the political artistic expressions of the mid-twentieth-century railed against the depersonalization and atomization created by large-scale political, economic and military systems. By the 1950s art had become packaged in a series of digestible styles and was beginning to become the gout of an emerging and newly educated middle class. Artistic culture responded by making itself inaccessible in an extreme abstractionism, but it was already too late. It had been overtaken by mass mediation and the limitless reproduction of artistic products. It could no longer claim an authority of taste but dissolved into a market place of styles. Avant-gardes had already destroyed any authoritative cultural tradition but now the syncretistic culture that they had promoted was left without legitimation.

The attacks on bourgeois values were not ineffective: the

productive individual was transformed into the expressive and demanding self; restraint was sacrificed to impulsive consumption; and a vocational commitment to work became *passé*. However, the chief culprit in the undermining of the spirit of capitalism (sometimes mistakenly called the Protestant ethic, or even more mistakenly called the Protestant *work* ethic) was its own invention. Easy credit, obtained through personal loans, instalment plans and plastic cards, enabled the rapid or even instant gratification of impulses. The moral justification for capitalism was not production but hedonism, and for Bell, hedonism cannot provide the unifying ties that bind a society together. The celebration of the individual leaves society without support.[3]

The decline of bourgeois values is bound up with what Bell calls 'the great profanation' in which modernity's stress on the moral authority of the self undermined the moral and existential certainties that had been provided by the great religions. Sacred religion was displaced by 'political religion' of which, for Bell, Marxism is the primary example, but within which we might include liberalism and socialism. However, the utopias they offered never came into view. Political religion joins the aesthetic of modernity as movements that successfully displace religion from culture but that cannot successfully satisfy the need that religion provides for. They offer neither meaning nor certainty but only a Nietzschean nihilism.

CONCLUSION

Steinfels (1979: 168) writes that what he refers to as Bell's methodological approach, the three-realms argument: 'probably deserves more attention from philosophers of social science and theoretically minded sociologists than it appears to have received'. One reason for its limited impact might be that a theoretical paradigm that distinguishes three or four sectors of society is not uncommon in theoretical sociology. Nor is it uncommon for the three (or three of the four) to be specified as the economy, the polity and the culture. Another might be that the formulation is not couched in an academic language of formal reasoning but in Bell's polemical and engaging, if somewhat journalistic style. The paradigm, once set out, is seldom elaborated but merely repeated.

In assessing the three-realms argument we can ask several fundamental questions. The first might be: 'Is society really

divided into realms?' Bell doubtless would disavow the salience
of this question because he claims that the paradigm is merely
an analytic tool that should be assessed in terms of its utility
rather than its validity. However, in so far as Bell argues that
modern society is beset by substantive disjunctions between
realms, the question remains appropriate. Indeed, he would not
need to fear the answer. There is so much sociological agreement
on the division of society into sectors that we can confirm the
validity of the approach. In complex societies there are quite
pronounced boundaries between the networks of social units
known as the polity or the economy that are recognized not only
by social scientists but by participants. However, it may be possible to speak of such realms only in relatively differentiated
societies where social units specialize in their activities. Elsewhere, as in, say, forager societies, the realms are best regarded
merely as analytic aspects of a unified society.

A second question might be: 'How many realms are there?'
In most sociological efforts to identify the sectors of society the
economy and the polity are relatively unproblematic. However,
matters become rather more confused when one seeks to categor-
ize the rest, the areas of culture, socialization, leisure, religion,
education, community and kinship. Clearly, all of these are outside the economy and polity and the alternatives are therefore
either to lump all or most of them together under such a heading
as 'latent pattern-maintenance and tension management' (L in
Parsons' AGIL scheme) or 'ideology' (as in Althusser) or to leave
most of them out and focus on aspects of interest. Bell does
the latter, confining culture to artistic expression and religion.
However, in so doing, he omits a whole realm of social life that
is focused on domesticity and community, and that both Schütz
and Habermas call the lifeworld. Indeed, this theoretical lacuna
may be the source of an endemic gender-blindness in the theoretical paradigm. Bell concentrates only on the public realms of
social life that have often historically been the exclusive domains
of men.[4]

A third question might be: 'Are the axes identified appropriately?' We do not need to address the axial patterns of culture
because they are specified tautologically. However, there is some
confusion about the axes of the TES and the polity. In what has
become something of a sociological orthodoxy, Weber specifies
that instrumental rationality is a widely pervasive aspect of
modern society and that its structural expression, bureaucratic

organization, originates in the state and spreads into other organizations. Bell, by contrast, has rationality, bureaucracy and unequal power firmly fixed in the TES while the state is a happy sphere of equality and democratic representation. Yet states, as opposed to the elective legislatures that form only a small part of them, precisely and primarily, are systems for the allocation of power in hierarchies that can be exercised authoritatively and even arbitrarily. An alternative to Bell might therefore suggest that the axial principle of the modern state is the monopolization of coercive power (in the police, courts and military) and its axial structure a system of bureaucratic surveillance. Reification would still remain in the TES but here the vehicle and thus the axial principle would be not rationalization but rather a commodification that extends beyond material objects to human labour and creativity. The axial structure for commodification is not the bureaucratic structure but the industrial one that combines human labour, machines and inanimate sources of power into a highly effective system of production.

The next question is: 'Are the realms disjunctive?' Answering the former question assists in answering this one. There is good reason to argue that Bell can only be committed to the idea of disjunctions between the realms of modern society because his specification of their principles and structures is inappropriate. For example, Bell's definition of culture that includes recursive attention to the existential problems of the human condition specifically allows him to question the validity of a commodified culture of hedonism *qua* culture. In fact, a conventional definition of culture does admit consumption culture. Similarly, his refusal to recognize that an enlarged state will be bureaucratized and will reify citizens as taxpayers or welfare recipients allows him to claim inconsistency between a democratic polity and a TES that subordinates and reifies people as wage-workers and consumers. Again, however, many sociologists would indeed argue that contemporary states are sources of unconstrained power and are entirely consistent with the constraints of employment.

The general difficulty is that Bell has fallen victim to what Holmwood and Stewart (1991: 42–4) describe as a 'horizontal' theoretical fallacy, a view that the contradictory elements of a theory are experienced separately in different parts of society. The contradictions enunciated by Bell lie not between the realms but between the different parts of his theoretical system, which, by implication, might be in need of revision. Societal realms must always be unified at the level of human experience. Indeed, modern society is surely one of the success stories of human history in terms of its capacity to survive, prosper and expand to near-universality. If it was riven by fundamental contradiction it would long since have disintegrated.

Lastly we can ask: 'How accurate is the history?' Again, the answer to the previous question gives us purchase on this one. We have seen that the idea of disjunctions may be problematic. A rather more convincing element of Bell's paradigm is the notion of crossovers, the idea that practices in one realm can influence practices in the others. Mobilizing this theoretical device one might seek to argue that, as the realms of modern society differentiate through time they become more interdependent, that is, the exchanges between them will become more frequent and intensive. The main historical proposition would then suggest a tendency towards consonance between the realms and the emergence of the familiar sociological picture of a Fordist TES, a corporatist state and a mass culture. Such a picture is scarcely disjunctive.

We can make a last point about how accurate the history is. As is noted above, at one stage Bell addresses the question of whether a corporatist state will ever emerge in Western societies. To a European observer this would look like a very odd question indeed. Bell's relatively undertheorized version of the modern state appears to be modelled on an idealized conception of what is specified constitutionally for the American state. Jeffersonian democracy may be virtuous in its institutionalization of emancipation but it has long since been corrupted and reorganized. Corporatist democracies have become the dominant pattern of political organization in Western societies. While the USA has been far less corporatized than other societies, even there the New Deal was indeed a corporatist arrangement between government, business and labour. More importantly, effective integration between these three elements is accomplished via the non-constitutional organs of the state, political parties and lobby and interest groups, with similar consequences to those found in Europe. Such a perspective leads us then to a fully-fledged alternative story of modern societies, such as that proposed by Habermas (1984; 1987), for example, in which humanity is besieged by threats to its freedom from an overly managed, rationalized and organized political-economic complex. Perhaps a balance needs to be struck between Habermas' critique of the *Rechtstaat* and Bell's apology for American idealism.

3

Labour and Capital

It is not altogether surprising that Bell's earliest sociological interest should lie in the area of work and its central relationship between capital and labour. Although he had abandoned communism and, along with it, his project for a Marxist analysis of the American state, the early part of his intellectual development was concerned intrinsically with such issues. Indeed, his subsequent ten-year stint as a journalist with that seemingly capitalist organ, *Fortune* magazine, was as Labor Editor.

Four features characterize Bell's analysis of economic life. First, as the previous chapter indicates, the economic arena is the arena of linear progress. Human beings are driven in the direction of technological innovation by an interest in maximizing their material welfare. Progress is linear simply because, once an innovation has been made, it cannot be lost unless the civilization within which it was created is utterly destroyed.

Second, Bell never abandons the negative, more or less Marxian, conception of industrial work that he developed in the early years of his career. As Chapter 2 shows, he was always convinced that the techno-economic sphere was the site of human subordination and hierarchy. Here he stands opposed to Weberian sociologies that propose that the political sphere is the arena of domination and subordination and that the economic sphere is an open market in which individual wants and aspirations can have free reign. For Bell, the source of liberating ideas is an open and active cultural sphere. And human beings can institutionalize the aspirations to freedom that they develop in cultural practices only within a democratic polity and not within the inevitably oppressive industrial economy.

Third, his view of American capitalism and of economic power is an expression of his anti-Marxism that stands in dispute with his socialist past. Nowhere does Bell view corporate economic power as arbitrary or as a source of class formation. Indeed, he takes the view that corporations are so internally differentiated and so subject to external controls that it is difficult if not impossible to locate any site of power within them. For Bell, power resides in concrete individual persons and groups rather than in abstract structures. Arbitrary economic power can therefore only occur under entrepreneurial or family capitalism in which an identifiable elite can own and inherit property.

Fourth, he takes a jaundiced view of the capacity of the discipline of economics to offer a fruitful analysis of economic life: 'economic theory is a convenient fiction, an "as if," against which to measure the habitual, irrational, logical, egotistic, self-interested, bigoted, altruistic actions of individuals, firms, or governments – but it is not a model of reality' (CET: 70). Even within such a model, it makes false assumptions about the individual maximization of utility, because it ignores the force of tradition and morality, and also about the freedom of markets that are everywhere constrained. For Bell, economic theory needs to take account of the formation of preferences within culture, of political practices and of long-term contextual trends. It needs to be tempered by the formulations of sociology and political science.[1]

WORK

Bell's first sociological piece on the character of work appeared in 1947 in the journal *Commentary* and is entitled 'Adjusting Men to Machines'. Here he reviews contemporary American research on the sociology of work located primarily within the 'Human Relations' school. Operating under the philosophical guidance of an Australian researcher, Elton Mayo, this research had investigated influences on the psychological adjustment of workers to industrial situations, with a view to engineering labour relations in order to maximize output. Bell engages in a trenchant critique of this Human Relations research by arguing that, in accepting business funding, researchers also accept business assumptions about the objectives of industrial work and about possibilities for the worker. They accept, he argues, the unstated assumption that the only criteria by which one can judge the value of work are mechanical efficiency and high output, and that they thus fail to consider whether work offers other possibilities for the expansion of human spontaneity and freedom. He accuses Human Relations research of an over-emphasis on empiricism and a neglect of theory, of a tendency to psychologize and individualize the problems of work at the expense of a macro-analysis that will identify the structure of the institutions of work, and of an insistence that workers are infinitely malleable in relation to any possible technology or work organization. Human Relations fails, for example, to examine the relationship between work and leisure, to investigate whether work can become as meaningful and enjoyable as leisure. And it resolutely insists that problems found in the workplace are the consequence of inadequate communication between managers and workers. Bell, by contrast, argues that the problem is not merely one of divergent understandings but of divergent interests, and that these interests must be accommodated if an industrial system is to be effective. Bell concludes: 'The belief in man as an end in himself has been ground under by the machine, and the social science of the factory researchers is not a science of man but a cow-sociology' (1947: 88).

The 'Adjusting Men' article then, sets a career task, to provide a macro-structural account of the development of the techno-economic sphere, what Bell is calling, at this stage, the industrial system. Indeed, he makes a first stab at theorizing this development that prefigures later arguments. The class system of American society, he argues, is being restructured. A new social stratum of technical and administrative employees is emerging focused on service employment. Simultaneously, the original working class is being downgraded by deskilling, by technological advances that tend to reduce its membership to the status of semi-skilled machine tender. The only way to get into technical-managerial occupations is to make an early decision to get advanced educational qualifications. However, those who fail to make such a decision are likely to suffer from levels of disadvantage and frustrated aspirations that in turn may lead to new militant attitudes that look nothing like the old trade unionism but that might be extremist, racist or anarchistic. Although this theoretical sketch is naive and inadequate, it specifies Bell's expanding interests – the growth of service occupations, the changing class structure and the sources of political extremism.

In a more extended piece, published some ten years later, Bell gives a more convincing account of the wider institutional development of work in which he is interested (WD; EI: 227–74). Broadly, for Bell like Weber, the development of work is a process of rationalization, of increasing levels of calculation of the relationship between cost and output. In a stunning formulation that prefigures both Foucault (1979)[2] and McLuhan (1964), he argues that this rationalization of work involves establishing a link between supervision and the formulation of metric time. The division of temporal experience into precise intervals by the use of clocks and watches allows calculations to be made of just how much effort any given worker is putting in. The contemporary enterprise, argues Bell, obeys three such logics, not only that of metric time but also those of size and of hierarchy, that stand in sharp distinction to the domestic experience of workers and that must be confronted by them under industrial conditions. The convergence of these three logics leads to the 'great achievement of industrial technology', the assembly line: 'the long parallel lines require a huge shed of space; the detailed breakdown of work imposes a set of mechanically paced and specified motions; the degree of coordination creates new technical as well as social, hierarchies' (WD: 10). The assembly line embodies what for Bell are the worst features of work, its monotony, drudgery and deskilling, and the subordination of the worker to machine control and close supervision: 'the worker, like the mythical figure of Ixion, is chained forever to the wheel' (WD: 23). The assembly-line worker is the victim of the cult of efficiency embodied initially in Taylorism and subsequently in Human Relations that seeks only to maximize output.

Bell concentrates on factory work because it is archetypal but he tries to show that its patterns spill out into other areas of work through the process of mechanization, 'because its rhythms, in subtle fashion, affect the general character of work the way a dye suffuses a cloth' (WD: 33). Mechanization extends back into such formerly individualized pursuits as underground mining and forward into the tertiary occupations of office work to turn them into the equivalent of factories. In an insight that anticipates Braverman's influential deskilling thesis (1974), Bell informs us that: 'In offices the installation of rapid high-speed calculators, tabulators and billing machines turns the white-collar workers into mechanically paced drones' (WD: 34). This means that every-where workers seek to escape work, by fantasizing alternatives, by changing their jobs, by aspiring to promotion, by concentrating on domesticity and leisure as the main sources of meaning in their lives, and by resisting supervision and control. They only work because their human spirit has been 'tamed' by the possi-bility of increased levels of consumption. Bell's industrial workers are instrumental in their orientation, focused on the possibilities offered by overtime wages, dual incomes and consumer credit: 'The desire for immediate gratifications – a car, spending money, a girl – burn strong.' (WD: 33).

Bell lastly considers whether transformations of the techno-economic structure will alter the character of work. Here he anticipates his own theorization of the post-industrial society as a service society (see Chapter 5). However, in WD he is much more circumspect than in the later publications. He admits that there is an increase in service occupations but his caution that the '*rates* of growth should not lead us into failing to consider the limited number of such positions available' (WD: 35; original italics) does not bear much comparison with the enthusiastic generalizations that can often be found in COPIS. Actually, Bell was much more interested at this stage in the possible conse-quences of automation for workers. He means by this machine processes that tend to eliminate human labour from the pro-duction process. Automation encompasses four developments: continuous flow arrangements for materials or components trans-fers; computerized data-processing; numerically programmed machine-tools; and mechanized assembly systems (WD: 47–8).

Bell adduces the consequences of automation as follows (WD: 51–4):

- the work-force will be transformed from a proletariat to a new salariat;
- the 'logic of size' will decline in importance so that plants will be smaller, geographically decentralized, and located closer to residential areas;
- diurnal work rhythms will change so that plants can operate

on a 24–hour basis and this will spill over into the consumption and leisure industries that service production workers;
- the self-conception of workers will change as production processes become more remote and mediated and as workers become masters of the totality of the job rather than some of its fragmentary elements; and
- work performance will also therefore become more difficult to measure in Taylorist metric terms and will have to be assessed qualitatively and holistically.

Bell leaves what he regards as the big consequence to the end, that of whether work itself will disappear, and if so, what happens to the individual and society. He is content, perhaps wisely, to leave that unrealistic question open.

UNIONISM

Among others, the previous chapter identifies a very significant contradiction between two of Bell's three realms. The principles of rationalization, reification and hierarchy that govern the techno-economic sphere contradict principles of participation, equity and justice that apply in the political sphere. This contradiction is fundamental to the constitution of trade unions precisely because they operate in both spheres. It is nicely captured, for Bell, in George Bernard Shaw's description of trade unionism as 'the capitalism of the proletariat', a description that is never more accurate than in America, where union leaders can simultaneously applaud the benefits of free enterprise and denounce capitalists as exploitative profiteers (EI: 211). As Bell confirms, the contradictions, of both constitution and rhetoric, are explained by the fact that unions operate in two contexts. In the political context they are social movements, mobilizing an ideology to try to reshape the social and political order. In the techno-economic context they are a market player seeking to influence the distribution of rewards to the maximum advantage of their members.

Bell can now characterize the American labour movement in terms of this contradiction. Put simply, it resolved the contradiction by defining itself primarily as an economic actor, by adopting an ideological stance known as 'Laborism', in which radical proposals were rejected in favour of power-sharing by means of bargaining and of lobbying for welfare legislation. American unions were able to persuade more liberal administrations to create a legislative context in which they could control the supply of labour by becoming exclusive bargaining agents. Indeed, American unions survive mainly in those industrial contexts where they were able to monopolize the representation of workers. The objective, in all cases, was to eliminate wages as a factor in competition between firms by means of such devices as 'pattern-bargaining' and industry-wide minimum wage agreements. The union thereby becomes intrinsically implicated in the fate of its industry because wage and profit levels will tend to rise and fall together. Hence the emergence of so-called 'business unionism' in which management and unions perceive themselves as having shared interests in the prosperity of the firm. Bell insists that this relationship is an uneasy one because each party has a residual tendency to identify itself and the other in class terms. However, it is reinforced by concertative action in the governmental arena, where business and unions often lobby on behalf of shared causes.

Bell's analysis of unions follows what will become a recognizable pattern. He lays out a set of analytic issues (here, the contradiction between economic and political principles), traces a history and then extrapolates from contemporary developments into the future. The history passes through four phases (EI: 217–18). Between 1860 and 1880 trade unions were primarily ideological social movements focused on class activism and party formation. Thereafter and until the 1920s there was a split between, on one hand, the American Federation of Labor (AFL), which, under Gompers, focused on the incremental improvement of members' material condition, and, on the other, such anarchosyndicalist groups as the Industrial Workers of the World, in which the AFL eventually prevailed because it was preferred by both management and workers. In the period immediately after the Great Depression, under attack from management interests, the AFL regained its ideological fervour, particularly under the aegis of an inner group of powerful unions, the Committee of Industrial Organizations (CIO), that eventually detached itself. Subsequently, during the Second World War and the cold war, unions joined the national opposition to fascism and then communism and thus ended its partisan action. The CIO was reabsorbed.

Bell can now move on to offer an assessment of contemporary prospects for American unionism. He makes four points, as follows (EI: 218–21).

- Union membership has reached its upper limit at about 30 per cent of the employed labour force. The reason it has reached this upper limit is that the great majority of union membership is in blue-collar occupations and these represent a declining proportion of employment.
- Unions are recognizing that collective bargaining is reaching the limits of its possibilities. The limits are defined by the level of national, industrial and enterprise productivity. These limits mean that collective bargaining takes place within agreed rules and is therefore subject to a process of bureaucratization.[4]
- The transformation of the proletariat into a salariat will alter orientations from class-solidaristic to individualistic.
- The union movement is experiencing organizational atrophy. Its leadership is ageing and it is losing its stomach for confrontation. Moreover, some unions are corrupt and associated with organized crime which tarnishes their public image.

These trends lead Bell, incorrectly on this occasion, to conclude that trade unions would reconstitute themselves as a social movement. They are moving away, he thinks, from direct representation and towards a symbolic status in which they 'stand for' the position of labour in public debates and governmental negotiations. In one sense they have no alternative to such a role because their membership is declining and they are being progressively excluded from formal negotiating rights in new industries. Curiously, in identifying the ideological content of this new unionism Bell shrinks from the possibility of a radicalization that would be consistent with its respecification as a social movement. Rather, he believes that it will become even more instrumental and 'embourgeoised', focusing on the national negotiation of standards of social services and quality of life. From the perspective of the 1950s Bell was also unable to predict that the successful politics of the end of the century was going to be a post-materialist politics. If labour was to be successful as a social movement it would have had to promote such causes as civil and women's rights, peace (especially in the Vietnam war period) and nuclear non-proliferation, and environmentalism. With the benefit of hindsight, we can say that if it ever did so its support was merely nominal. Against Bell's prediction, the American union movement embraced conservative positions, even partly allying itself with the Republicans, and as a consequence slid into ever deeper obscurity.

Bell has an opportunity to revise his argument about trade unions in the 1970s (COPIS: 143–54; see Chapter 6). In broad terms, however, he does not want to change his mind. His projection of the stagnation of the movement is confirmed, and its cause is the reconstitution of the labour force in the direction of more service occupations. The union movement has failed because the underlying class system that sustained it has decomposed, because collective bargaining does not suit industries that are not profit-orientated, and because women and blacks are difficult to organize. We might argue that the union movement might have survived better had it addressed the issues that were significant for female, black and middle-class workers rather than retreating into a palefaced and patriarchal conservatism. For Bell these are not cogent issues.

CAPITAL

We can view Bell's three contributions to the analysis of capital as a historical sequence. The first (EI: 39–46) analyses the transition from family to corporate capitalism in America towards the end of the nineteenth century; the second (COPIS: 269–98) examines the structure and functions of the corporation in the contemporary period; and the third (1993) projects the decomposition of large corporations. Bell's view of corporate capital is clearly conservative (in his own terms 'liberal'), in as much as it denies that large corporations or the elites that run them are fundamentally powerful, but it is not apologetic. Bell remains directly critical of the Lukácsian capacity of corporations to reconstruct human beings into objects by using what he calls 'economizing' practices.

In a formulation that is reminiscent of Engels, Bell begins his analysis of capital by looking at the social structure of the family (EI: 39–46). The family rests on the linked institutions of property and dynastic marriage. Property gave power to families and dynastic marriage ensured that any such property that was accumulated by a family remained within it. This link between family and property was the foundation of the class system: 'people met at the same social levels, were educated in common schools appropriate to their wealth, shared the same manners and morals, read the same books and held similar prejudices, mingled in the same milieus – in short, created and shared a distinctive style of life' (EI: 40). The source of the general breakdown of the dynastic marriage system, in an extension of the Engelsian formulation, is romantic love and the release of passion. In Bell's sexist terms, the fact that women could marry across class lines meant that the family hold on property was seriously weakened.

In the colony society of the USA, family capitalism never took as firm a foothold as it did in Europe: capitalism was managerialist in orientation quite early; land could be bought and sold in the market rather than being linked to family inheritance, and there was an early tradition of intergenerational mobility. Nevertheless, family capitalism did take root in the merchant and manufacturing groups of New England and elsewhere on the Atlantic coast and in the *ante-bellum* South. In fact, the rapid industrialization that took place after the Civil War was initiated by individual entrepreneurs and family groups. They founded what Bell calls the 'middle-sized' industries in food and brewing, chemicals, publishing, textiles and banking. The system broke down around the turn of the twentieth century when an undercapitalized, or as Bell puts it an 'overextended', American industry went through a series of crises. Control of many firms passed into the hands of bankers who reorganized them as shareholder corporations and installed professional managers to run them. Bell insists that such managers, who often came from engineering backgrounds, sought their rewards in status and power rather than money and wealth – the Ford and Rockefeller families were exceptions in a system in which it was not normally possible to inherit corporate control.

The giant corporations that were created by these managers were a 'new social invention' (COPIS: 276). They were able to institutionalize, to an ultimate degree, the 'economizing mode' of social action, action that is committed to maximizing productivity by an increasingly efficient use of resources. Bell takes as his example of a great economizer, Alfred P. Sloan, the first chief executive of General Motors Corporation and the inventor of what is now known in organization theory as the 'divisionalized structure' (COPIS: 276–8). Sloan broke the organization down into a series of operating divisions each with its own separate budget and each with its own product line. Each unit of product could then be costed and costs could be controlled by central inspection of each division's capacity to provide a return on the capital that was invested in it. Costly or inefficient parts of the corporation could no longer 'hide' by passing on costs to other divisions.

Bell is critical of the economizing mode because it is internal in its orientation, failing to take into account such externalities as the public provision of infrastructure and an educated workforce, the costs of cleaning the environment and the necessity to provide for 'public goods' as well as private consumption.[5] He believes that these criticisms have become so widely accepted that we must now assess the performance of corporations under the terms of what he calls the 'sociologizing mode' of action. The sociologizing mode combines notions of social justice with a commitment to providing public goods and a consequent expansion of the public sector. Corporations can expect, he argues, to face taxation penalties in circumstances where they fail to provide social justice or in which they create public costs. Bell is quite convinced that, in the second half of the twentieth century, corporations began to move away from the economizing and towards the sociologizing mode (COPIS: 287–9). They have been reconceptualized as social organizations of people and the site for much of each person's lifetime experience rather than simply as a means for the production of goods and services. They are no longer exclusively committed to profitability and now pay much more attention to quality of working life and employee loyalty.

With not a little hindsight, for Bell this development was 'historically inevitable'. As the traditional institutions of community, church and family have declined, the corporation has become the focus for social aspirations to status, security and justice. Corporations can conspire in a much more humanistic approach to employees that supports such aspirations precisely because employees, rather than stockholders, have become its main source of capital. Although theoretically corporate capitalism involves risk-taking investment by entrepreneurs, in fact most capital is raised by the internal generation and reinvestment of funds. This in turn depends on the labour, the skills and the knowledge and ideas of its employees. Ownership is therefore a legal fiction because shareholders do not control the operation of corporations. Rather, their status is more akin to that of a lender: 'the corporation may be a *private enterprise* institution but it is not really a *private property* institution' (COPIS: 294). Corporations are actually possessed by their employees.

Bell proceeds to draw an analogy between the emerging business corporation and the university in which the management and the board of directors are theorized to be equivalent to university trustees. They hold the corporation in trust, certainly for stockholders, but also for workers, consumers and the public at large.[6] In all of these terms, then, the contemporary corporation is becoming 'subordinated', subjected to external influence and internal democratization, so that it is ceasing to be the determining institution of society.

Perhaps these changes will be accelerated by developments in the economizing mode itself. In a recent journalistic piece, Bell (1993) forecasts the downfall of the large-scale, divisionalized organizations that Sloan invented. Curiously, they appear to be the victim not of social innovation but of technological development: in the three cases that he discusses US Steel is defeated by the oxygen furnace and the mini-mill; GM by computer-integrated manufacturing; IBM by the invention of the personal computer. On this new evidence the subordination of the corporation is occurring as the consequence not of phenomenological increases in the scale of society, of the recognition that there are public as well as private goods, but of the operation of the market. In an era of rapid technological innovation and shifting patterns of demand, smaller, more flexible and flatter companies can succeed against Fordist (or perhaps 'Sloanist') dinosaurs. In an interesting reversal of Marx's theory of competition, the 'small capitals' appear to be beating 'the large'.

CLASS

Bell's interpretation of class derives from his life-long dialogue with Marx.[7] For him, Marx's concept of class as a division based on property ownership is most useful in the analysis of Western industrial society between 1750 and 1950, a period in which the new industrial bourgeoisie and proletariat were able to displace the old feudal status orders of nobility and peasants. Bell interprets this development in a scheme derived from Durkheim that divides any society into a series of 'vertical' situses – landed agriculture, the church, the military, the legal system, the mercantile system – that are vertical in that they run from the top to the bottom of society in stratification terms. With the emergence of highly effective industrial technologies and organizational principles the economic situs 'swelled up' (increased its power) so that its commodifying values pervaded all the other situses and its class system became the predominant social division. He therefore rejects Marx's argument that human history is the history of class structures, and instead confines class to a particular period of history.

This still leaves some problems, however. First, Marx did not himself use the term class in a consistent way. Bell identifies five different usages: as a rhetorical device to indicate any oppressive system, as a latent structure, to discuss fractions of the historic classes, as part of the abstract modelling of the capitalist mode of production and as a set of empirical divisions in contemporary society. This problem of usage is compounded by the fact that in contemporary sociology class has taken on several other possible meanings: as divisions based on occupation or authority, as positions in credit, commodity or labour markets, or as sociable groups marked off by rank, status or subcultural attributes. To this Bell might have added the possibility of treating classes as collective political actors operating through the party system and trade unions.

Bell's solution is to detach the idea of class from any particular foundation. Rather, it can be based on any of three sources of societal power, property, skill or political position (COPIS: 361; cf., Wright 1985). As his analysis of family capitalism confirms, Bell argues that access to property takes place by means of inheritance or entrepreneurial ability. Skill is mediated through the family although it is unclear why Bell should think so in view of the fact that it is better thought of as accessed through education and is mediated by the talents and performances of the individual. Political position is acquired by election or co-optation and as mediated by membership of an interest or ethnic group. Unless it is subsumed by political position, nowhere does Bell include the possibility of class formation on the basis of managerial authority and subordination that derives from the control of large-scale organizations and that is independent of educational qualifications.[8] However, his own definition of class can now emerge, but in providing it, and in line with his absolute commitment to social constructionism, Bell insists on a *für sich* component. A definition of class must encompass both an institutional source of social power and a 'cultural outlook' providing a common consciousness and a legitimation for the existence of a class. He confirms then that, 'a "class" exists when there is a community and continuity of institutional interest and an ideology that provides symbols of recognition (or codes of behavior) for its members' (WP: 155).[9] Thus, the capitalist bourgeoisie was assuredly a class, 'because of its community of interest in the system of private property, the continuity of the system through the family, and the justification of private property through the system of natural rights' (WP: 156).

Using this set of defining statements Bell can now move on to argue that the class structure of contemporary capitalist society is undergoing a transition. In broad outline, property is of declining importance as the basis of class and power, and skill and political position are of increasing importance. The origins of this view are to be found in his argument about the break-up of family capitalism (EI: 39–45) that disempowers inheritance as the factor that locks in property as the key social determinant. The consequence, for Bell, is that there is no longer a ruling class in society in the Marxist sense. There remains an 'upper class' that enjoys privileges and can pass these on, but this upper class does not constitute the political elite or ruling group. Moreover, this upper class is separated from a 'managerial class of function' that cannot pass its positions on by inheritance (WP: 156).

Although we might dispute the accuracy of Bell's analysis to this point, we cannot dispute its clarity – the class structure of modern capitalist society becomes increasingly differentiated and complex so that we can no longer speak of a single, ruling, culturally dominant class in a way that has often been attributed to Marx. However, Bell's analysis of developments after 1950 with the emergence of the post-industrial society is marked by a contradiction that reveals a deficit in analytic precision. In one piece (WP: 144–64; first published in 1976) he accuses the purveyors of the concept of a 'new class' of 'muddled' conceptualization. This piece is consistent with the above discussion – class becomes more complex but starts to disappear after about 1950. The 'knowledge stratum' that might form the basis of a new class encompasses various occupations including scientists, teachers, artists, mass media workers, social service workers and managers. However, these occupations are distributed across highly differentiated situses (business, government, universities, social-service organizations and the military). Since situses are the bases for interest formation, the knowledge stratum cannot constitute a class. It is therefore, 'questionable whether the amorphous bloc designated as the "knowledge stratum" has sufficient *community* of interest to form a class, in the sense understood for the past 150 years' (WP: 157; original italics). Bell concludes, 'if there is any significance to the idea of a "new class" ... it cannot be located in social-structural terms; it must be found in cultural attitudes. It is a mentality, not a class' (WP: 161).

A firmer conclusion could not have been reached. Yet in COPIS (374), published at about the same time, Bell makes it equally clear that, 'the major class of the emerging new society is primarily a professional class, based on knowledge rather than property'. Indeed, in his typical workmanlike way, he lays out all the statistical dimensions of the 'knowledge class' (COPIS: 213–21). Bell makes clear, at one level, that the knowledge class is more like a status group than an industrial class. He speaks of it as being made up of estates and denies that it has a coherent identity. However, he insists on continuing to use the term 'class' to describe it.[10]

CONCLUSION

We can begin to see in Bell's analyses of labour and capital the personal contradictions that represent both the strengths and the weaknesses of his subsequent sociology. He has confined his socialism to the sphere of work, arguing that only there are applications of power and domination effective. However, his political liberalism leads him into comments on the development of capitalist organizations and of class that can only be regarded as apologetic. Thus, the statements on capital and labour cannot be regarded as the strongest elements in Bell's oeuvre.

The key problem in Bell's analysis of work is that he seems to have accepted the Marxist definition of capitalist work as dehumanizing and degrading without also accepting the possibility specified in the early Marx that work can be creative and liberating. Certainly, he criticizes Human Relations for its incapacity to recognize these possibilities, but he appears himself to be the victim of a similar misperception. The techno-economic sphere is intrinsically, axially hierarchical, objectifying and alienating. It admits no possibility of democratization, enskilling, participation and meaningfulness. Such a critical-socialist stance is unhelpful in that it fails to arm those who are the victims of such practices but it is also apologetic in so far as it implies that managers have no alternative but to engage in them. The post-industrialization of the techno-economic sphere should call for a reinterpretation of work but Bell cannot reconstruct his position without denying the axial principles that he has set out in the three-realms argument.

This fundamental constraint translates into each of the other elements of Bell's argument covered in this chapter. His treatment of the development of American labour unions in the direction of a non-activist and apolitical instrumentalism is couched broadly in a tone of approval. Nowhere, for example, does he address the abject failure of these organizations to protect the relative living standards of anything other than a very small minority of American workers. The protection of the working class as a whole can only be accomplished by political action. In his own rejection of ideological extremism Bell fails to recognize the possibilities offered to the advancement of workers' instrumental interests that might have been offered by a moderate social democratic party. Nor, as I have said, does he seek to analyse the extent of patriarchalism and anti-minority practice in the American labour movement.

The analysis of the development of American capitalism verges on the bizarre. The root of the problem appears to be a fixation on the heritability of property and its associated privileges. Bell is saying, in effect, that one cannot find an unfair or unjust distribution of property and power so long as they are not heritable. This leads to the view that the executives of large corporations are not disproportionately propertied, are not inordinately powerful, do not constitute a class and are not excessively privileged simply because there is no direct inheritance of position. At a minimum, this view needs at least to take into account the vast literature on the social reproduction of class membership. More cogently, no class theorist has ever claimed that class membership depends on inheritance, this characteristic being reserved for feudal estates. Bell paints an unlikely picture of giant corporations as wimpish weaklings subject to the arbitrary constraints of governments and consumers and to the demands of their employees to turn them into model employers. Indeed, the picture of the subordinated collegial corporation contradicts the earlier statements he has made about the cult of efficiency in American business.

Lastly, Bell is weakest in the area in which we might expect a sociologist to be strongest, that of class. Putting not too fine a point on it, Bell appears either unable to distinguish class from general socio-economic inequality or, where he does, unable to stick with his own definition. This is confirmed by the fact that he goes through exactly the same analytic and empirical steps in different publications to arrive at radically dissimilar conclusions.

Bell needs perhaps to avoid loose usages of 'class' and stick to a single definition. In the end this would probably lead him to a confirmation of the more accurate of his two positions, the one specified in WP, that argues that the post-industrial society is a society without classes. He would then be able to develop a more precise analysis of stratificational developments that focused on the concepts of status-group and estate that he also employs.[11]

4

The Exhaustion of Political Extremism

If Bell's early radicalism and later journalism had inspired an interest in the problems of labour and capital it had also stimulated an interest in political sociology. Without engaging in *ad hominem* judgements, we can here begin to see Bell's intellectual reconciliation of his prodigal past. His long encounter with socialism had left him with a profound impression of its incapacity to make a significant impact on American political life. In 1949–50 he embarked on a history of American socialist politics that addressed the question: 'Why did the socialist movement, as an organized political body, fail to adapt to the distinctive conditions of American life as did, say, the British Labour Party in England?' (MS: vii). Here he introduces many of the themes that were subsequently to inform his more explicit political sociology: the failure of ideology in the face of pragmatics; the decline of class politics and its displacement by status politics; the uniqueness of American political parties relative to their more ideologically suffused European counterparts; and the relative underdevelopment of the American state. Bell's political analysis proceeds from the failure of Marxian socialism in the United States; to analyses of the emergence of McCarthyism in the 1950s; to an argument that suggests that the USA presents a general exception to the radical ideological currents that swept Europe; to an extension of this argument that suggests that ideology is no longer the central dynamic of politics in any Western society; and finally to a liberal conception of the state in which status-claimants are criticised for their refusal to subordinate their interests to the pursuit of a common good.

THE LEFT

Twentieth-century organized socialism in America is represented in three main movements: the Socialist Party that became especially active in the 1930s; the Communist Party that saw its main period of strength during and immediately after the Second World War; and the labour union movement that was the most successful of the three in establishing itself as an institutional force. However, none of them was able to institutionalize itself as a viable political alternative. The Socialist Party had, for a time, run many American cities, including cities as large as Milwaukee, but it never elected a US Senator or a state governor. In the post-Second-World-War period its electoral support declined to insignificance and any influence it exercised thereafter was felt through its absorption into establishment positions in the unions, the 'liberal' wing[1] of the Democratic Party, liberal pressure groups and public service positions.

Bell shows that the Communist Party and the labour movement represent opposite poles in organizational strategy and success. The Communist Party was founded just after the First World War and throughout its life was the victim of state harassment and repression. It tended to operate outside conventional electoral politics, in Bell's version, as a conspiracy that sought more or less to advance the interests of the Soviet Union. It was most successful during the Second World War when communism was allied with capitalism against fascism. Even then, however, its principal activities were carried out through 'front' organizations promoting 'peace' or friendship with the USSR. By contrast, the American labour movement was the most organizationally successful of the three main worker political movements, organizing up to 30 per cent of American employees (EI: 218). However, it accomplished this by separating itself from politics. It divorced itself from socialist affiliations as early as 1900 and it never sponsored a political party in the way that European labour movements did, that is, by direct financial levies on members and executive participation. Indeed, it was not itself highly centralized in the way that those organizations were. While it was closely associated with the Democratic Party, especially by way of financial contributions, it was never organically linked to that party.

Traditional explanations for this failure focus on the exceptional circumstances of American industrial life. Bell addresses, in particular, Sombart's explanation for the lack of class consciousness in terms of the fluid nature of American labour and the early establishment of the universal franchise, and Kayserling's explanation in terms of an egalitarian Americanism, unique to that culture and its historical circumstances (EI: 276–7; MS: 3–4). However, each falls back on an argument that material abundance saps workers' political energies and commitments. Bell quotes Sombart's exclamation that: 'On the reefs of roast beef and apple pie socialistic Utopias of every sort are sent to their doom' (in EI: 277). He seeks his own explanation in the character of the labour movement itself.

Bell's explanation for the failure of an ideologically committed socialism in the USA is couched in terms of a central dilemma between ethics and politics. The ethics of socialist movements involve a general critique of capitalist society and its institutions and an argument for their displacement in favour of a Utopian vision of a future society based on equality of contribution, condition and power. The politics of such movements involve decisions about whether to participate in capitalist political institutions, whether to accept the minor victories of reform or to hold out for the ultimate triumph of revolution, and whether to collaborate in alliances with other progressive forces in order to elicit broad support or to remain pure and solitary in opposition. Bell argues that American socialism failed to resolve this basic dilemma, although a more accurate rendition of his position might be that the movement failed to effect a compromise between politics and ethics by insisting on a Utopian moralism. For Bell, it is indeed a failure:

> [T]he socialist movement, by the way in which it stated its goal, and by the way in which it rejected the capitalist order as a whole, could not relate itself to the specific problems of social action in the here-and-now, give-and-take political world. In sum: it was trapped by the unhappy problem of living *in* but not *of* the world; it

would only act, and then inadequately, as the moral, but not political, man in immoral society. It could never resolve, but only straddle, the basic issue of accepting capitalist society and seeking to transform it from within, as the labor movement did, or of becoming the sworn enemy of that society, like the Communists. [EI: 278–9; original italics]

A religious movement can keep its organizational commitments within the secular world and reserve its moral commitments for the sacred, but a political movement like socialism cannot do this.

The political reality that the socialist movement needed to recognize was that working people were fundamentally orientated not to a socialist Utopia but to improving the immediate conditions of their material existence. Bell sees the Socialist Party as being 'in the world' in so far as it recognized this. Indeed, it proposed specific reforms that would offer such advances. But in refusing to accept the reality of the political system within which such reform would, in the absence of Utopia, have to take place, it was not 'of the world'. The Party remained pacifist and isolationist in both world wars. It refused to support Roosevelt's Keynesian New Deal policies, and submerged itself in a continuous, internal, factional and ideological feud rather than genuinely seeking power. Indeed, Bell argues that 'the back of American socialism was broken' as early as the First World War, when it failed to support American intervention (EI: 287)

Unlike the Socialist Party, the Communist Party was neither in the world nor of it. Its particular difficulty lay in maintaining each of these postures while simultaneously transforming the world. It accomplished this by alienating itself, by becoming a secret society, distant from and in an adversarial relationship with bourgeois institutions. It was able to avoid participation by allowing its front organizations to undertake political action, and indeed to mobilize and incorporate liberal interests. But Bell shows that this strategy equally was doomed to failure. In alienating itself, the Party established itself as a stranger, an outsider of American life and an easy target for those who sought to stereotype it as an 'unAmerican' activity. American communism was successfully repressed long before it could become redundant.

By contrast, Bell views the labour movement, particularly the American Federation of Labor (AFL), as a success because it had learned to live both 'in and of the world'. In particular, Bell lionizes Gompers, the founder of the AFL, for his wisdom in electing to restrict union activity to collective bargaining for wages. In so doing, Bell argues, the labour movement succeeded in displacing traditional American commitments to individualism in favour of an acceptance of collective action (MS: x). However, here Bell's analysis must be regarded as somewhat weak because the industrial action undertaken by the AFL did not displace individualism but rather reinforced it because collective bargaining served the ends not of the solidarity of a class but of the sumptuary interests of individual workers. In claiming that the AFL satisfactorily resolved the dilemma Bell misses the point that it resolved it by suppressing ethics in favour of politics. As he shows elsewhere (EI: 211–26), the AFL was divided from more ideologically committed sections of the labour movement, the syndicalist Industrial Workers of the World and its successor the Conference of Industrial Organizations, before defeating them and later absorbing them on its own terms. The American labour movement has long since ceased to embrace a socialist ideological commitment, and in these terms must be viewed as part of the failure of Marxian socialism to take root and not as a successful alternative. It practises what Bell calls 'market-unionism' and others call business unionism, it endorses enterprise-level bargaining, and it has never sought to modify the distribution of ownership and decision-making in industrial enterprises.

In a retrospective on his analysis of socialism in the USA Bell integrates that earlier formulation with his subsequent and more famous proposal about the end of ideology (see below). Here he states his position explicitly:

> [A] set of ideological blinkers prevented the American Socialist Party from understanding society. To state the paradox most forcefully: the American Socialist Party, though often called reformist or right-wing, was actually a Marxist party. [MS: viii]

Bell here confounds a commitment to ideology in general with a commitment to a Utopian and unrealizable Marxist ideology in particular. Throughout his analysis it is unclear whether it is the former or the latter that prevents the formation of popular support. We can explore this issue further in addressing Bell's analysis of an altogether different political group.

THE RIGHT

If Bell was concerned about the failure of socialism to shed its ideological blinkers and engage in a pragmatic programme of reform, like many other liberal intellectuals he became positively alarmed about the emergence of a radical and fundamentalist right wing in American political life in the 1950s. The most public manifestation of the increasing impact of the right on American politics was the emergence of McCarthyism, named after Senator Joe McCarthy, chairman of a congressional committee on 'unAmerican activities'. McCarthy was a classic witch-hunter who sought to root out the evils of the communism that was sapping American strength wherever he could find it. Naturally, he found it wherever he looked for it, and he principally looked within the intellectual and cultural elites of science, academia, literary life and, most famously, the Hollywood movie industry. Bell concedes that the Communist Party had had an influence in these areas far disproportionate to its actual membership, that genuine spies and infiltrators had been exposed, and that the Soviet Union, a recent ally, had become surprisingly aggressive. None of this, however, could explain to him the McCarthyite generation of a compulsive Americanism that perceived threats in institutions as diverse and innocent as the Girl Scouts and the Voice of America (RR: 57–8).

The clues to an explanation of the emergence of McCarthyism can be found, argues Bell, in an examination of McCarthy's supporters. They included the disenchanted sons of former patrician rulers; status-threatened new rich entrepreneurs and wheeler-dealers who opposed heavy taxation; the rising ethnic middle class including Irish and Germans who sought to prove their patriotic commitment; and a small group of intellectuals, themselves often ex-Communists exercising the zeal of the convert. Bell mobilizes an idea from Hofstadter (in RR: 75–96) that suggests that McCarthyism represents the emergence of a new 'status politics'. Hofstadter argues that, just as *déclassé* groups express status anxiety through political behaviour (an explanation often invoked to explain the rise of European fascism) so also may rising status-groups. Such a configuration is likely to emerge under conditions of advancing prosperity. Because such status-groups are both anxious and unacculturated the patriotic response is likely to be 'amorphous and ideological' (RR: 58–61).

Bell's personal contribution is not an attempt at explaining the emergence of McCarthyism but rather at explaining its success. He grounds this in a particular feature of American life that he calls 'moralism'. Moralism emerged from a clash between the unrestrained character of frontier expansionism, a middle-class, Protestant emphasis on respectability cultivated in small-town America and an egalitarian and anti-intellectual evangelism among splinter Protestant groups. The compromise of American moralism is to tolerate political corruption and economic exploitation but to impose a rigid code of personal conduct and cultural censorship. McCarthyism is, for Bell, an attempt by small-town and evangelical America to moralize politics. The moral fervour of the attack, the demonization of the opponent by labelling, the resentment against liberal control of the cultural establishment, could only be maintained because communism was equated with sin (RR: 61–70).

In a later reflection (RR: 1–45) Bell turns his attention to the emergence in the early 1960s of radical-right action groups that threatened what he regarded as the fragile American political consensus by fighting communism using communist methods. Three instances of right-extremism raised the alarm: the John Birch Society, a conspiratorial, neo-fascist organization; the spread of week-end seminars and schools run by revivalist preachers to expose the secrets and the evils of dialectical materialism; and the formation of guerrilla warfare training groups preparing themselves to defend America from Soviet invasion, of which the best-known example is the Minutemen, named after a nuclear ballistic missile designed to respond to Soviet attack within a four-minute warning period.

Maintaining the theme that such developments represent a moral crusade on behalf of small-town, Protestant America, Bell shows that in attacking communism the radical right was also able to attack not merely liberal intellectuals but also intellectualism in general, as well as taxation, the welfare state and the entire corpus of bureaucratic expertise. All of these were seen as threats to basic virtue and thus all were branded as communist. The real enemy comes into Bell's view:

> What the right wing is fighting, in the shadow of Communism, is essentially 'modernity' – that complex of attitudes that might be defined most simply as the belief in rational assessment, rather than established custom, for the evaluation of social change – and what it seeks to defend is

its fading dominance, exercised once through the institutions of small-town America ... [RR: 16]

Bell explains the re-emergence of right-extremism during the
1960s by invoking an argument that prefigures his later and more
famous claims about the cultural contradictions of capitalism
(CCC; see Chapter 7). American culture was founded in ideas of
achievement, 'masculine optimism' and progress – the USA had
won all its wars, was economically dominant and had the 'biggest'
and the 'best' of everything material. The 'American style' therefore consisted of three unspoken assumptions: 'that the values of
the individual were to be maximized, that the rising material
wealth would dissolve all strains resulting from inequality, and
that the continuity of experience would provide solutions for
all future problems' (RR: 18–19). This consensual value system
underlay a political system in which various sectional groups
(regional, ethnic, etc.) traded, dealt and bargained with each other
to realize their interests in a series of *ad hoc* arrangements that
kept the state weak. In the 1960s the political system came under
threat from extremism precisely because the American style was
threatened by new international developments: European economic performance began to outstrip America; the USA managed
only a doubtful performance in the space race against the USSR;
American military adventurism proved less triumphal than in the
past; and America was cast in the role of a neo-colonial power.
But, for Bell, certain internal changes cast greater doubt on the
integrity of the American style: individual action was displaced
by the collective activities of labour unions, farmers' organizations
and pressure groups; *ad hoc* bargaining led to a dearth of planning
in the provision of basic services, especially in inner municipal
areas; and foreign policy was beset by an inability to make a
realistic assessment of its possibilities. Traditional Americanism
had entered a crisis and those with most at stake in it moved to
defend it.

In a reversal on his earlier position, in which he showed
right-extremism to be the property of rising status-groups, Bell
now argues that it becomes the ideology of groups marginalized
by the march of history, what he calls the 'dispossessed' or declining status-groups. He identifies three particular dispossessed
groups:

• the generationally dispossessed, the small-town, fundamentalist

Americans no longer able to affect policy in Washington because of the entry of the technocratic new-dealers;
• the dispossessed managers, business executives who experience a tension between their power within the corporation and their inability to effect national policy in its entirety; and
• the dispossessed military, those senior officers without the political skills and the technical knowledge to influence military policy.

Right-extremism represents a coalition of these groups exercising a primitivistic ideology in which they seek to reassert traditional American values and power structures in the face of a technocratic and bureaucratic rationalism.

THE CENTRE

For Bell then, the left and the right equally exhibit a dangerous tendency: 'The tendency to convert issues into ideologies, to invest them with moral color and high emotional charge, invites conflicts which can only damage a society' (RR: 71). The American polity is focused on a non-ideologically formed and more or less stateless centre. Importantly, for Bell, this is not only a matter of fact but a matter of value-preference. Having examined the threats we can now move on to see how Bell conceptualizes the political centre.

Bell subsumes his analysis of the centre of American politics within a recurrent theme of American exceptionalism, the idea shared by many Americans that theirs is an especially great and important society (WP: 245–71; 1989). The important fact that he sees as contributing to this view is that, perhaps uniquely, the USA is, or was, the complete civil society. The USA was formed as a motley mix of human flotsam from Europe who constructed an open society in which each 'man' could engage in individual self-realization and advancement. American society was never organized from the top, and partly as a consequence, was riven by violent class struggle of an intensity and extent seldom witnessed in Europe. Nevertheless, these struggles, as we have seen, were not about capturing the state but merely about material returns to labour. Indeed, there was no state to capture, only a government. In an important formulation Bell conceptualizes the government as a political market place, an arena in which interests can compete and deals can be struck. The rules of the market place are established by the Supreme Court which is the 'bedrock' of civil society (1989: 50) (a peculiar formulation given that it is part of the state). So American political culture is materialistic, in the sense that it involves bargaining between moneyed interests, and populist, in so far as it combines individualism with egalitarianism.

Bell insists that the party system in the USA was resolutely ideological (WP: 264). However, each of the main political parties represents multiple ideological shadings and cleavages rather than being constructed around a single ideological (or class) division. The effect was to disempower ideology, because partisans were always obliged to make compromises if they were to accomplish their aims. Moreover the cleavages cross-cut one another. The cleavages of class that set farmers against financiers and employees against employers were cross-cut by status-group cleavages between small-town traditionalism and urban modernism. These cleavages are further cross-cut by cultural preferences. For example, labour unions, the Southern plantocracy and liberal intellectuals all tend to support the Democrats, but the liberals are very different from the other groups in terms of their cultural radicalism. For this reason, American political parties are coalitions of interests rather than ideological social movements.

Bell shows that the combination of a weak state with interest-coalition parties was the dominant pattern until the 1930s. The first change in this configuration was the growth of the state during the New Deal and Second World War periods. Bell attributes these developments to three causes (1989: 53–5). The first of these is the growth in the scale of society so that business corporations and other organizations were now operating on a national and international level. Economic and fiscal policy also therefore had to operate on that level. Second, there was a re-alignment of the sectional interest groups that supported political parties so that now the Democrats had the support of organized labour, farmers and ethnic minorities. Each of these was interested in government regulation and subsidization so that Democrat influence tended towards an expansion of the state. Third, the imperatives of military mobilization during the Second World War became the 'forcing house' of the state. On the other hand, Bell insists that the superpower foreign policies of the second half of the century did not carry similar imperatives to centralization. There was indeed a spread of subsidies and entitlements in relation to defence procurement, but this was organized in relation to regional interests rather than central planning. However, despite the fact that 'there was never really a unitary national state' (1989: 54), 'the problem of "the State" has become central for American political theory and practice' (1989: 55). Even in the USA, the state, for Bell, has become too big, too distant and too inflexibly centralized to deal with societal or individual problems.

Meanwhile, domestic politics has taken what Bell regards as a dangerous turn. The party system is the victim of partisan disalignment and the breakdown of party patronage systems in the face of the advance of popular claims for entitlements. In place of partisan politics, the American electorate has focused on large single issues – in the 1960s these were the Vietnam war, race relations and an emerging culture of permissiveness linked to inner-city social pathologies. For Bell this presages a possible political re-alignment[2] but he is rather more concerned about the general distrust that is increasingly accorded to the political arena. Americans, for him, appear decreasingly willing to compromise and thus increasingly likely to polarize. This raises, for him, the dangerous prospect of 'a crisis of the regime' that will entirely destabilize the American political system.

THE END OF IDEOLOGY

A curious feature of Bell's political sociology is that its central and most controversial idea is not of his own origination. Bell (EI: 411) himself notes that the phrase, 'the end of ideology' was first used by Albert Camus in 1946. It entered sociology in the hands of one of Bell's intellectual confidants, Raymond Aron, who wrote a chapter entitled 'The End of the Ideological Age?' for his book attacking Marxism called *The Opium of the Intellectuals* (reprinted in Waxman 1968: 27–48). Aron gave a thematic address to a conference of the Congress for Cultural Freedom in Milan in 1955 where several notable liberal and conservative intellectuals (including Edward Shils, Karl Polanyi, Hannah Arendt, Anthony Crosland, Richard Crossman, Hugh Gaitskell, Max Beloff, José Ortega y Gassett, Sydney Hook, John Plamenetz, John Kenneth Galbraith, Colin Clark, Seymour Martin Lipset and Bell himself) rehearsed the idea. Bell's contribution to the conference was a piece on America as a mass society (EI: 21–38) that does not mention the end of ideology. Bell selected the theme as the title for a collection of essays on class and politics published in 1960 but addressed it explicitly only in an epilogue. Bell himself admits: 'There are some books that are better known for their titles than for their contents. Mine is one of them' (EI: 409). This is by way of saying that Bell's name became the most recognized in relation to the argument and he has, perforce, remained the chief apologist for it (see EI 409–47; 1990b).[3] His entry into the 'end of ideology' debate is an exhibition of his capacity to tune in to the intellectual mood of a period and to crystallize the issues in a comprehensible, if polemical, form that stimulates and guides the central debates.[4]

Waxman (1968: 5) sums up the end-of-ideology thesis in two premises: first, it specifies the disappearance of ideological politics in modern, Western societies, especially in the USA where 'there almost never was an ideological age'; second, that this development is value-positive because ideology prevents the construction of a good and progressive society. Aron's original version of this thesis addresses three types of ideology – nationalism, liberalism and Marxian socialism. Nationalism is weakening, he argues, because the nation-states are weakening as they become economically and militarily interdependent and because of the emergence of superpowers that are imperialistic rather than nationalistic. Liberalism is failing because it cannot offer a sense of community as a focus for commitment. Meanwhile, Marxian socialism, the 'last great ideology', is failing because it is false. It was proposed as an ideology for the proletariat but it was actually promulgated by bourgeois intellectuals as part of their last battle in their war with aristocracy. One can witness the consequences in state-socialist societies where ordinary workers continue to be oppressed and exploited by a 'bourgeois' (presumably in the French meaning of 'professional middle class') ruling elite. In summary, Aron argues that the social-structural underpinnings of ideology have disappeared.

> The once unequivocal distinction between 'right' and 'left' ha[s] been damaged by the knowledge that combinations once alleged by extremist doctrines to be impossible – combinations like collective ownership and tyranny, progressive social policies and full employment under capitalization, large-scale governmental controls with public liberties – are actually possible. [Shils in Waxman 1968: 52]

Against this background, Bell offers two arguments about the exhaustion of ideological partisanship; the first empirical, the second theoretical. The former is the most influential and is the one on which we shall concentrate here.[5] Ideology is, for Bell, a secular religion: 'a set of ideas, infused with passion' that 'seeks to transform the whole way of life' (EI: 400).[6] Ideology performs the important function of converting ideas into social levers. It does so precisely by that infusion of passion, by its capacity to release human emotions and to channel their energies into political action, much as religion channels emotional energy into ritual and artistic expression. But for Bell, religion is more effective than ideology because it can help people to deal with that imperative fundamental of human existence, death. Even so, the secularization processes of the nineteenth century constructed a general psychical vacuum. Ideology was partly able to fill this gap by emphasizing the continuity of collective triumph (e.g. the thousand-year Reich) against individual mortality. The political ideologies of the nineteenth century were also strengthened by two important alliances: with a rising class of intellectuals seeking to establish status against lack of recognition by the business bourgeoisie; and with the positive values of science that could measure and indicate progress.

'Today', Bell asserts, 'these ideologies are exhausted' (EI: 402). He gives three causes:

- the violent oppression carried out by socialist regimes against their populations;
- the amelioration of the worst effects of the capitalist market and the emergence of the welfare state; and
- the emergence of new philosophies that emphasize the stoic-theological ontology of humanity as against romantic philosophies emphasizing the perfectibility of human nature.

Bell's conclusion is captured in the following passage:

> [O]ut of all this history, one simple fact emerges: for the radical intelligentsia, the old ideologies have lost their 'truth' and their power to persuade.
> Few serious minds believe any longer that one can set down 'blueprints' and through 'social engineering' bring about a new utopia of social harmony. At the same time, the older 'counter-beliefs have lost their intellectual force as well. Few 'classic' liberals insist that the State should play no role in the economy, and few serious

> conservatives ... believe that the Welfare State is 'the
> road to serfdom'.... [T]here is today a rough consensus
> among intellectuals on political issues: the acceptance of
> the Welfare State; the desirability of decentralized power;
> a system of mixed economy and of political pluralism. In
> that sense too the ideological age has ended. [EI: 402–3]

Bell is not, it must be stressed, entirely triumphalist about this
development. He mourns the spent passions of intellectualized
politics and wonders how the energies of the young can be channelled into them. And he also pleads for the retention of Utopias
as focuses for human aspiration, because without them society is
reduced to a meaningless materialism.

In an afterword written in 1988 for the republication of EI
(409–37), Bell adduces five criticisms that were levelled at the
book and answers them thus:

- EI was a defence of the *status quo* because it denied the
  possibility of an opposition to capitalism, pretending that none
  such was needed. Bell replies that there is no *status quo*, no
  capitalist monolith. Indeed, all he would ever wish to defend
  is democratic socialism, since he is opposed to the reifications
  of capitalism.
- EI promoted technocratic guidance at the expense of political
  debate. As Bell points, out he has always called for an
  advanced level of political debate.
- EI denies the possibility of moral discourse. Bell's critique of
  the vacuity of contemporary secular morality is well known
  (see CCC). The criticism confounds moral discourse with ideological discourse when they are clearly not identical.
- EI was an instrument of the cold war. Bell cannot make sense
  of this critique (which comes from Wright Mills), and indeed
  it is incoherent.
- EI was disproved because of the advance of ideology in the
  Third World and because of the student radicalism of the 1960s.
  The first charge, as Bell rightly indicates, is nonsense because
  his epilogue is entitled 'The end of ideology *in the West*'. Within
  it he even offers an extensive commentary on the current and
  prospective development of Third-World nationalist ideology.
  He spends rather more space on countering the other criticism
  that focuses on student radicalism. The New Left student
  movement was, for Bell, not an ideological movement at all
  but a moralizing movement focusing on such issues as the

Vietnamese war but without a coherent political philosophy. Its unifying theme was liberation but it had no commitment to traditional partisan enterprises and no plan for the reorganization of economy and society.

Bell takes heart from the fact that none of the critical comments challenged his central argument that Marxian socialism was no longer relevant to the analysis of contemporary society (EI: 421), but this involves a slight misreading of his own work.[7] Although Marxism is the issue most centrally on Bell's mind, his analysis was clearly intended to apply to *all* ideologies and not just to Marxism. The surprising feature of Bell's self-defence is that he does not address the problem of the emergence of the radical economic fundamentalism that featured in the Reagan and Thatcher regimes of the 1980s. The recasting of the Republican and Conservative Parties respectively in an ideological mould that rejected the intellectual consensus on the welfare state and mixed economies would surely present the most serious challenge to his thesis. That reconstruction was certainly partisan, it was certainly passionate and it certainly involved a new philosophy of economic life.

THE PUBLIC HOUSEHOLD

We can now turn to an examination of Bell's interpretation of the contemporary polity. That view is structured by the two themes discussed so far: the early relative weakness and subsequent enlargement of the American state; and the absence of a structuring ideological partisanship in American politics. Drawing on a term used in some areas of economics, Bell argues (CCC: 220–82) that the polity should be reconceptualized in sociology as a 'public household'. The state has enlarged so much that it has become a principal arena ('realm') of economic life to stand alongside the domestic household and the market economy.

> The public household, as expressed in the government budget, is the management of state revenues and expenditures. More broadly, it is the agency for the satisfaction of public needs and public wants, as against private wants. It is the arena for the register of political forces in the society. [CCC: 221]

He uses the term 'household' because it connotes the problems

of shared living arrangements that one finds in families, of recon-
ciling common advantage with individual advantage.[8] Just as
the private household seeks to meet the material needs of individuals, the public household seeks to meet the common or collective needs of society, 'to provide goods and services which
individuals cannot provide for themselves' (CCC: 224).

Traditionally, this provision has extended to military protection, diplomacy and colonization, transportation infrastructure
and basic education. Recent expansion of the state has changed
the character of the public household. It has taken place in three
main areas (CCC: 225–6):

- the assumption, by the government, in the face of the Great
  Depression, of the functions of economic allocation, redistribution, stabilization and growth;
- government sponsorship of science and technology, directly
  and through the universities, in the 1950s; and
- government commitment in the 1960s to redressing economic
  and social inequality through such policies as civil rights, housing provision, health care, and income support.

The public household has therefore become reconstructed and
expanded to such an extent that is now beginning to dominate
both the private household and the market economy. The public,
he argues, now views the state as the arena for meeting not only
collective needs but also individual needs and private wants. The
public household has thereby become a political market in which
claims for the realization of such needs and wants compete. The
problem is that the transfer of provision from the domestic and
market spheres to the state has left such claims without constraint,
which leaves the public household in a fiscal crisis.

Bell can now move on to discuss the consequences of this
expanded competition for public entitlements. This expansion
involves the intersection of two well-recognized processes: the
expansion of rights through the institution of citizenship by which
states sought to legitimate their sovereign power; and the revolution of rising expectations that was founded in the consumption-
led expansion of corporate capitalism. This, Bell argues, has led
to a revolution of rising entitlements involving, say, guaranteed
incomes, minimum education or government-funded health care.
Bell insists on the full meaning of the word 'entitlements', that
is, that these are not simply claims for redistribution to the disad-
vantaged but for all members of society. The provision of govern-

mental services has expanded correspondingly. This raises two problems for the state. First, there is a structural imbalance between the private and public sectors, such that, given that labour represents a higher proportion of costs in the public sector, any inflation of wages and any expansion of services in that sector will represent a drain on the public purse that will be difficult to sustain. Second, there will be an increasing overload and centralization of issues that the decision-making structures of the state will find it impossible to manage.

Such an analysis of the public household represents for Bell an example of 'fiscal sociology', a term he derives from Schumpeter, that means an analysis of the balance of social forces that impinges on the costs and revenues of the operations of the state. The main problems of his fiscal sociology are summed up in the following passage:

> The sociological fact about modern Western democratic polities is that the political system is a wider arena within which all kinds of interests – ethnic, economic, functional (e.g. military), bureaucratic – are claimants. The political and philosophical problem of the public household derives from the fact that the state has to manage the double function of accumulation and legitimation: to provide a unified direction for the economy, in accordance with some conception of the common good ... and to adjudicate ... the conflicting claims of the different constituencies. In its first task, it has the autonomous function of leading and directing; in the second, it is at worst an arena of power, at best a normative umpire. [CCC: 231–2]

It is clear that for Bell the public household is experiencing a tension between these two functions. The function of accumulation, the pursuit of economic growth, cannot succeed without investment. Private investment depends on low taxation, and public investment would equally require the diversion of resources from meeting entitlements and other claims. Moreover, growth depends on advances in consumption and these tend to fuel inflation. Under inflationary conditions people tend to save less which in turn reduces investment fund liquidity. However, the function of legitimation cannot proceed without the economic growth that allows governments to reward their clamouring constituencies. Under these conditions there has occurred a crisis of political belief, resulting in what Bell calls a loss of *civitas*: 'that spontaneous willingness to obey the law, to respect the rights of others, to forego the temptations of private enrichment at the expense of the public weal . . . [i]nstead, each man goes his own way, pursuing his private vices, which can only be indulged at the expense of public benefits' (CCC: 245).[9] This loss of public responsibility is felt most keenly in the area of taxation. If the meeting of entitlements serves to increase taxes to high levels, this will not only cause discontent but such practices as tax avoidance and tax revolts that will actually reduce fiscal capacity to meet entitlements. Bell is particularly concerned about the fate of the middle class under conditions of high inflation and high taxation. The middle class is withdrawing its support from politics and contributing to the partisan disalignment discussed in the preceding sections. It raises the spectre with which Bell is haunted, of the prospect of political extremism and the undermining of democratic institutions. Again Bell demonstrates a remarkable prescience because there was a shift to the right in Western politics in the 1980s that, if not extremist, was certainly radical.

In the most general terms Bell recasts these dilemmas in relation to the three-realms paradigm (see Chapter 2):

> The economic dilemmas confronting Western societies derive from the fact that we have sought to combine bourgeois appetites which resist curbs on acquisitiveness, either morally or by taxation; a democratic polity which, increasingly and understandably, demands more and more social services as entitlements; and an individualist ethos which at best defends the idea of personal liberty and at worst evades the necessary social responsibilities and social sacrifices which a communal society would demand. [CCC: 248–9]

Bell now moves to propose a liberal political philosophy that will restore a normative commitment to the public household and provide a basis for the mediation of private conflicts. In brief, this political philosophy embraces four issues:

- The *cui bono* issue, that of the units in terms of which the society should be specified and therefore of who should be the beneficiary of its operations. Bell rejects all of the three separate possibilities – individuals, intermediate groups and the state – because to endorse any one of them would threaten either liberty, or the public good or genuine aspirations. His solution is that the public household should recognize the rights of all individuals and all interest groups. However, as he has argued himself, the delivery of such recognition involves impossible trade-offs.

- The liberty-equality, or liberalism vs. socialism issue, that of how much the state should regulate behaviour in order to achieve equality. Here Bell expresses little fear about liberality because 'today most of the disparate outcomes of status, income and authority are justly earned' (CCC: 264). If we leave aside the contestability of this claim, we can focus on Bell's philosophical response. He argues that inequality between individuals should only prevail where individual differences between them that are relevant to the sphere of activity prevail. Thus money should not be the determinant of access to education; ability should. And nor should money be the basis of access to health care; corporeal need should. In a parody on Marx, he concludes: 'If our criterion ... is the reduction of undue and illegitimate influence and command of resources, the relevant principle of liberty and justice would be: to each according to his earned effort; to each according to the powers and privileges appropriate to each sphere.' (CCC: 269).
- The equity-efficiency issue, that of how much non-economic values should enter into standards of performance. Here Bell argues that the questions of consumption, investment and conservation cannot be centred on the individual but must be regulated in terms of the social and future good. He does not help us by telling us how far individual behaviour ought to be regulated, how much the 'social discount' should be.
- The public-private issue, that of how much the state should intervene in private economic and moral decisions. Here Bell endorses *laissez-faire* principles, specifying that a competitive economy is more productive than private or public monopolies. Indeed, he extends this into welfare areas, where he suggests that services should be provided by private agencies competing for public finance. He also endorses a strict moral distinction, a bourgeois hypocrisy, between public and private spheres of morality as the only liberal possibility.

These arguments, although often indecisive, are clear in what they reject. They reject what Bell calls 'bourgeois hedonism', the reign of unfettered appetites in the market, and they also reject the illiberties of state planning and regulation. They also reject the unfreedoms of economic oligopoly. He seeks to maintain individual liberty, appropriate rewards for effort and merit, and commitment to labour and investment. In a strikingly illiberal pose, he argues that the arbiter of these cannot be the market because the market carries no principle of justice. Rather the arbiter must be the public household.

CONCLUSION

Bell's political sociology can be read as a history of the American polity. It begins with the social construction of an idealized polity in which the state is subordinate to civil society and in which material interests are held to be legitimate. Political action is not driven by lofty goals and thus the political parties that are formed are not built around ideologies but around expediency. They may, however, accommodate numerous ideological positions within their factions. This happy state lasted until after the First World War when exogenous developments forced some shifts. The state expanded rapidly, taking on a bureaucratic and technocratic character. The impressive character of these great events also encouraged the emergence of parties of the ideological left. However, these were unable to adopt a sufficiently pragmatic orientation to appeal to material interest-groups. In the second half of the century, ideologues of the right engaged in political action as a fundamentalist response to the burgeoning bureaucratic-technocratic state. These failed in the face of a general trend towards the decomposition of ideology brought about by a consensus on the welfare state and a minimum level of regulation of the economy. But the end of ideology itself provokes a crisis of political commitment and a danger that the polity will experience wild and unstable swings of support and contestation as single issues grip the collective psyche. Bell's solution is a recommitment to the principles of liberal public sphere.

This history reflects all of Bell's personal commitments and fears, even where some of these may be contradictory. For example, he rejects ideology but fears nihilism; and he is committed to individual freedom but only if it is channelled morally and productively; and he simultaneously embraces liberal humanism and rigid Calvinistic commitments to thrift. This means that his political sociology is incomplete and thus partial. First, it is a political sociology of *America*. It is not an analysis that can easily be applied to, say, Sweden or Italy, the former highly corporatized, the latter ideologically partisan. So it does not inform us about the way in which polities work in general, only the way in which one polity has evolved. This can be defended on the grounds that that was all Bell intended to do; indeed, that he writes explicitly of the exceptional character in American politics, but he also insists on generalizing. He writes of the end of ideology *in the West* and proposes the public household as a general political philosophy. The political sociology of the USA might have benefited from the employment of more explicit comparative analysis.

A second criticism is rather more important. Steinfels (1979: 176) accuses Bell of constructing an antiseptic image of politics, 'at most a civics-text creation'. This is not wholly accurate. In RR, for example, Bell mentions the manner in which American morality accepts political corruption. Indeed, a person who grew up in a poor area of New York City in the 1920s would be overwhelmingly aware of such corruption. The problem is that Bell does not build the issue into the sociology, rejecting completely, for example, Mills' contention that America is run by a ruling elite and asserting that with the corporatization of capitalism there is no such thing as managerial or business power (interview 9/11/94). It is as if all the claimants in the public household stand outside legislative and executive processes without penetrating and influencing them. The influence of defence contractors, farmers, gun-runners, and drug-dealing tobacco producers extends far beyond that of the simple claimant and is able to affect legislative processes against clear majorities of public opinion. Moreover, the American political system has managed progressively to exclude those weak claimants who provided a threat of fiscal drain by using the (liberally philosophized) requirement for proactive voter registration to disenfranchise them. The danger of an overtaxed public and a bankrupt state no longer exists, unless as a consequence of demands for ever more sophisticated 'toys' for the military. This can be witnessed in the recent failure of the American political system to deliver the sort of universal health-care entitlement that all other modern societies take for granted.

We have seen that in his analysis of American exceptionalism Bell was prescient enough to recognize that issue-politics held out the threat of polarization. That polarization indeed arrived in both the USA and Britain during the Reagan–Bush and

Thatcher–Major regimes. The principle strategy in each case was to cultivate a political basis for support by the creation of two nations; the first was rewarded for productive enterprise, lightly taxed and morally conservative, the second was depressed and unsupported, exploited where possible in deregulated employment contexts and stigmatized as morally and economically feckless. Bell would doubtless deplore the departure of such a strategy from his own vision of a public household, which is a one-nation strategy. The problem is that the development occurred not out of issue-politics but out of a combination of liberal (i.e. libertarian) economic extremism and moral fundamentalism. This was indeed a restoration of liberalism, but not one that fitted Bell's model. More importantly, it represented a return of divisive ideological politics of a type that Bell believed had disappeared for ever.

Despite these flaws, Bell's political sociology has much to offer. His conceptualization of the weak American state and its relationship to civil society provides a useful lever on current moves in the direction of disétatization and privatization (although he also fails to consider these developments in any serious way). His willingness to take a definite public position in the end-of-ideology debate crystallized that exchange and led to its reception as a serious contender in the arguments about the shape of contemporary politics. Above all, the construction of the argument on the public household is a model combination of clear analysis with philosophy which ought to be, in that famous publicity phrase much beloved by publishers, essential reading for any student of political science. It puts the case for left-liberal commitment to the society as a community that involves contributions as well as claims with utter conviction and parsimony and stands against the extremist individualism of economic rationalism.

5

An Excursion into Education

One of the least known of Bell's sociological interests is in the structure and functions of education, especially of higher education. As Chapter 6 shows, he eventually reveals this interest almost as a passionate commitment in the 'post-industrial society', where his belief in the virtues and possibilities of the university leads him perhaps to overstress its capacity to determine the future shape of society. However, that interest had developed rather earlier. In 1963 the Dean of Columbia College,[1] David Truman, asked him to form 'a committee of one' to spend a year reviewing the undergraduate curriculum. The review was subsequently published as a book (RGE). This truly was an excursion into the field because Bell probably never intended that education was to be a centrepiece of his sociological contribution.

The book emerged at a time when university education in particular was in turmoil. It had expanded under the weight of the post-war baby boom and the students were of a generation that had experienced comparative affluence, freedom from exposure to major international conflict and relative freedom of expression. The USA became embroiled in a post-colonial war in Vietnam that brought it into contest, if not outright conflict, with its opposite superpower, the USSR.[2] The war could not be won and was also ideologically unacceptable on the left. Many young American men resisted or avoided conscription and many students, especially in the major universities, became politically active. The consequent political mobilization addressed not only the Vietnam war but spread over into wider issues including civil rights and the democratization of universities. Bell did not hesitate to join the arguments, publishing an analysis of the student revolt at Columbia (CSRU: 698–107) and a paper on the governance of the universities (1970).

Bell's personal assumptions about the position and importance of education in society are given in the Columbia review (RGE: 144–78). He believes that education should be liberal, that is, open in the opportunities that it offers and in providing individuals with the chance to discover their own identity in relation to the stock of human knowledge, rather than doctrinaire or inculcative, that is insisting that their identities should be cast from a common mould: 'It can liberate young people by making them aware of the forces that impel them from within and constrict them from without' (RGE: 152). Bell specifies the content of liberal education more closely through six purposes (RGE: 152):

- to overcome intellectual provincialism, that is, both the myths, ideologies and biases that people can hold by virtue of their formative experiences and the narrow specialization that can be acquired by training in a particular expertise;
- to engender an appreciation of the place of conceptual innovation in the advancement of human knowledge (here Bell prefigures the emphasis on theoretical knowledge in COPIS);
- to develop an awareness of history because it provides points of comparison and cross-reference;
- to show how ideas relate to social structure;
- to foster an understanding of the value-relevance of social enquiry; and
- to demonstrate that the humanities have a civilizing effect.

The undergraduate curriculum that Bell recommends reflects both these commitments and his own experience. For example, in a proposed 'Civilizations' course, all students must begin with an examination of ancient civilizations (he was himself an undergraduate classics major), all students must do some history and all students must be exposed to at least one social science.

We can now move on to examine the sociological aspects of Bell's accounts of education.

A CHANGING SOCIAL CONTEXT

Bell's account of the changing social context of education is a combination of arguments drawn from his analysis of politics (see Chapter 4) and his theory of the post-industrial society (see Chapter 6) that hypothesizes an increasing importance for theoretical knowledge.

The political development he sums up in the idea that the USA has recently 'passed from being a nation to becoming a *national society* in which there is not only a coherent national authority, but where the different sectors of the society, that is economy, polity, and culture, are bound together in a cohesive way and where crucial political and economic decisions are now made at the "center" ' (RGE: 69; original italics). Here Bell adduces several issues that will have become familiar (RGE: 69–73). One is the increasing level of government spending, especially in the defence industries, and the increasing proportional size of the federal budget; another is the way in which the federal government commits itself to specific national policy goals, such as full employment. Such commitment implies fiscal management by the manipulation of taxation and interest rates.

Alongside this national economy there is also developing a national polity by the extension of citizenship rights into the socio-economic arena. The New Deal of the 1930s had ensured that the federal government had begun to assume many of the powers that previously had been vested in the states and the city governments. This process was extended in the 1960s as the government sought to engineer social equality by means of civil rights, anti-discrimination and voter-registration legislation and its enforcement. Such moves were supported by an extension of welfare-state provisions including medicare, social security, welfare payments, housing, environmental protection and education itself. A particular feature of these developments was an attempt to include minority groups, especially blacks, in political and social processes that previously had been dominated by big business, the migrant ethnic political machines of the Northern cities and the labour unions. However, the increasingly centralized character of American government was not only a construction of laudable domestic developments. As we have seen, Bell attributes a major impetus to American participation in the global war of 1939–45 and the leading position that the USA took in the victorious alliance in that war. The fact that the USA remained alert to a perceived Soviet military threat during the succeeding cold war created a large, permanent and centralized military and intelligence establishment. That military establishment in turn cultivated a federally orchestrated process of scientific and technological research primarily committed to defence needs. In 1963, 60 per cent of the 2.5 million technical specialists in the USA were employed on federal funding.

Bell's third and last aspect of the emergence of a national society is the development of a national culture. This centres on the growing intellectual class of the universities and the capacity of its members to move in and out of Washington policy circles as the political hue of the government changes. More importantly, this national intelligentsia is increasingly linked together by electronic and mass communications that increase its collective consciousness. Mass communications, especially television, have also contributed to the emergence of a national popular culture in which the sentiments and emotions of a large proportion of the population can simultaneously focus on a single event or entertainment. This might be a Super Bowl football game but it might equally be the assassination of a president or minority riots in an inner city.

The post-industrial-society themes in Bell's account are discussed in finer detail in Chapter 6 of this book. In brief, he makes four points in relation to education (RGE: 73–87):

- that knowledge is growing exponentially so that the stock of its material manifestations (books, articles, words, etc.) are accumulating at an increasing rate;
- that knowledge is also rapidly differentiating, 'branching' into multiple fields and subspecialities;
- that an important recent development is the emergence of a new intellectual (i.e. non-physical) technology, e.g. game theory, decision theory, simulation, linear programming, cybernetics and operations research, that are transforming social science by improving its capacity to model, forecast and project; and
- that there has recently been a major expansion in research and development involving large increases in the expenditure of human resources and government funds.

Society is therefore becoming more future-orientated and more planning-orientated. The fit of the education system to the knowledge society therefore becomes apparent. In the past economic expansion could be promoted by capital investment but in the knowledge society it must be promoted by educational and scientific investment, by investment in human capital. The problem is that the returns to human capital are paid out on a 25-year cycle. The imperative for a future-orientation therefore comes at least partly from education itself.

SECONDARY EDUCATION

Many analyses of the social organization of secondary schools argue that there is a hiatus between, on one hand, a pro-school set of behavioural patterns that engage middle-class students, the high academic performers and teachers and, on the other hand, an anti-school syndrome that focuses on working-class students and popular culture. Bell's view of high-school social organization is much more critical, perhaps more jaundiced, than this. First, he argues that within all adolescent cultures academic achievement counts for very little (RGE: 111–12). Student peer cultures tend negatively to evaluate able students and even to stereotype them as deviant (in an older argot as 'squares', in a more recent one as 'spocks'). Rather, students tend to reserve positive evaluation for those who are popular and sociable: athletic and car-owning boys, and attractive girls. Against conventional wisdom that this is a *sub*cultural feature, Bell argues that it is actually an extension of predominant adult popular culture. In an analysis that recalls his discussion of the important early influence of small towns in American life (see Chapters 4 and 7) he argues that this is because the local high school is often an important focus for community participation, especially in so far as athletics is concerned, where the high-school football or basketball team can often come to be seen as representative of the community as a whole and where the PTA is the main community organization. Thus, high-school popularity becomes symbolic of community status, reflecting back on the parent and contributing to the arrangement of the local pecking order. The consequence is an informal conspiracy between parents and students that militates against intellectualism and academic achievement of a cosmopolitan kind.

The second aspect of Bell's sociologically based critique of secondary schooling (RGE: 112–14) is more akin to the deschool-ing criticisms of the left than the elitist criticisms of the right. For the small-town critique he had drawn on Coleman and Berger but here he draws on Friedenberg. The result is reminiscent of his Marxian critique of the reifying consequences of capitalist industrial production systems (see Chapter 3): 'If predominant student values militate against intellectualism, the oppressive atmosphere – almost one of policing – in many of these schools tends to herd the students into tight routines' (RGE: 112). In part this is clearly a bureaucratic requirement, an attempt to preserve order and to protect public property from the hedonistic ravages of the young. But, in a passage that calls to mind Bowles and Gintis' work, Bell also sees it as an element in a much wider, perhaps more sinister agenda: 'It is part of a more pervasive, if unplanned, effort to harness the young into the organizational features of the adult world' (RGE: 113). This organizational 'har-ness' has two components: an elaborate structure of pseudo-adult activities, focusing on preparation for work and family formation; and an emphasis on planning one's college education and sub-sequent career. This leaves the adolescent young without a 'time-out', a period free from adult pressures when they can find their own identity and express their personal style. Bell interprets Bohemian, beat(nik) and hippie subcultures as reactions to organ-izational regimentation that could be avoided if such a time-out were available.[3]

Given the societal importance ascribed to secondary edu-cation and its lack of success in meeting its own goals, in large measure due to these built-in structural factors, centralized attempts to reform it became frequent. Bell examines four such reform programs (RGE: 110–11, 114–39):

- *Curriculum reform.* Here Bell is generally positive about attempts in mathematics and science to develop more 'heuris-tic' curricula that emphasize student verbalization, personal discovery and experimentation. He is deeply critical of the need for reform of the English curriculum that too frequently offers popular fiction rather than the 'canon' and of social studies where schools appear to teach whatever they wish to teach.
- *The 'Advanced Placement' and 'Early Admissions' programmes.* Under these programmes, schools could offer college-level courses to enable the students that took them to sit for an

'advanced placement' test taken prior to college entrance. This enabled them to move directly into second-year courses (of a four-year degree) on entering college. Broadly, Bell argues that these have advantages for schools in so far as they tend to open up and decentralize curricula by developing an academic stream, and in so far as they promote the development of a pro-intellectual culture, but they have disadvantages for the colleges because they mix students at different stages of their development and because they reduce the possibility of the student receiving a first-year general education.

- *Teaching improvement.* The major innovation is the introduction of 'fifth-year' add-ons to the B.Ed. to allow a concentrated specialization in a teaching subject, usually in the form of an arts degree (e.g. the MA(Teaching) at Harvard).
- *Interdisciplinary courses.* The development of broad humanities and social studies courses to replace disciplinary specialization, especially in private high schools. For Bell this dilutes knowledge and prevents detailed study.

Taken together, the above reforms represent for Bell a major change in the pattern of secondary education. The traditional pattern is a 'comprehensive' one in which age-cohorts are exposed to a common curriculum and progress through the school as a single cohort. The emerging pattern is one of ability groupings ('streaming') within schools and differentiation between elite or specialized schools and general or mass-education schools. However, Bell proposes that there are limits to such reforms imposed by the intrinsic nature of different disciplines. Here he proposes a tripartite division that bears a resemblance to the three-realms argument (see Chapter 2) that must be more than coincidental. Some disciplines (science, mathematics, languages) are relatively objective and sequential, involving students in solving puzzles at various stages and allowing them to move forward in measurable steps. Others (humanities) are 'concentric' or cumulative, in which major themes (e.g. death, love, tragedy) are recursively revisited in different expressions. Yet others (social science) are 'connective' restlessly exploring the linkages between various phenomena and their contexts. Only the first of these can genuinely be accelerated because these are the only disciplines that involve a linear progression. In a prediction confirmed by subsequent events, Bell argues that any attempt at interdisciplinary humanities or social science courses in the high schools is for him, in one of his favourite terms, merely 'modish' and likely to fail (RGE: 139–42).

THE UNIVERSITY

Bell identifies four functions that are performed by the university (1970: 61–2):

- it is a custodian of the (Western) cultural tradition and the arbiter of status within it;
- it searches for truth through research and scholarship;
- it trains people for professional occupations; and
- it applies knowledge to social and community uses.

He specifies two models of the university that stress different aspects of these functions. The first, the 'classical' model stresses the first two functions. A commitment to these includes a claim to the right to speculate on and criticize any matter free of external political or commercial interference. However, crucially for Bell, it also involves the responsibility of maintaining this posture entirely at the level of theoretical as opposed to practical discourse. The second or 'pragmatic' model involves a stress on the last two functions and, by implication, because Bell does not say it, a withdrawal from rights of academic freedom because the university is serving the interests of the political and commercial organizations that pay for its services.

In 'Quo Warranto?' (1970: 63) Bell argues that society must choose between these two models, either as a generalization throughout society or on a university-by-university basis. However, in RGE he makes clear that the choice might already largely have been made: 'The university today, whether private or state, has come to be a quasi-public institution in which the needs of public service, as defined by the role of the research endeavor . . . becomes paramount' (RGE: 88). He traces this development through the establishment of government sponsorship of military and scientific research laboratories, rises in government spending on tertiary education, the development of policy research institutes in social science, the differentiation of elite graduate schools from liberal arts colleges and the changing role of the academic. He also reintroduces post-industrial-society themes: the university becomes the main source of technological and social innovation; whether and what type of university education one has will determine one's place in the stratification system; a majority of the population will attend; almost all specialized occupational training will be carried out in higher education; higher education will become a continuing lifetime involvement; and the university will be the centre for cultural life and expression (RGE: 106–7). Thus, 'the universities are now in the process of a great transformation, carrying out multivaried functions which educators never dreamed of' at mid-century (RGE: 94).

The consequences and pressures for the university are as follows (RGE: 275–7):

- They are no longer institutions for the elect and the able but must cope with a wide range of student abilities. More importantly, they must create academic distinctions between various experiences and performances.
- The number of talented students has not increased so there will be an increased level of competition between elite universities to recruit them.
- The graduate school has expanded in size and influence relative to the undergraduate college. This tends to drain human and financial resources away from undergraduate teaching, especially in so far as status distinctions emerge between the two.
- The university has been transformed from a *Gemeinschaft* to a *Gesellschaft*. Student protest and drop-out is founded on, 'the impersonality of a university, its rushed and dispersive quality, and the lack of "encounter" between student and faculty – not just personally, but in a moral and intellectual sense' (RGE: 276).
- The university operates in a global context. Universities are increasingly assessed in terms of their contribution to national standing in global military and economic contests.
- Hyperdifferentiation in science multiplies the number of subjects and courses that a university must teach.
- The university is the central institution of the society: it must be the source of innovation; it must allocate status; and it must train specialists. This makes it a nodal point of pressure between governmental regulations, commercial interests and the expectations of students and parents.

In these points then Bell confirms that the 'classical' model no longer predominates. Universities are service institutions providing research, expertise and training to external bodies. Because government largely pays for these services they constitute an important claimant constituency, a lobby group that forms an important part of the educational policy community. The internal consequences are sharp. Previously, the academic system of governance was collegial in character, but now it is largely bureaucratic. In the process, teaching and the authority of the teacher have reduced in importance.

Bell concludes RGE (307–11) with what might be his most heartfelt comment. In a rehearsal of an argument that is to become increasingly important (see Chapters 2 and 7), he identifies the major threat to the traditional academic pattern as the disjunction between social structure and culture. Education, and particularly higher education, is being pulled apart by opposing forces, the reifying rationalizations of an increasingly post-industrial techno-economic structure and the independent development of a postmodernist culture that stresses experience and individual preference in opposition to performance and duty. This disjunction is expressed in a tension between two types of orientation to the future, technocratic and apocalyptic. The technocratic orientation is instrumentally rationalistic:

> The technocratic view distrusts ideology; emphasizes the discipline of mind and the discipline of fact; is orientated to problem-solving; and employs an increasingly powerful armory of intellectual techniques to enlarge the means for controlling nature and to sharpen the definition of the rational conduct of men. [RGE: 307]

Technocratic professionals envisage a unidimensional future that is orderly and rational and that drives out opinion and expression. The alternative apocalyptic view is expressed in the postmodern sensibility that, 'seeks to abolish constraint by substituting experience for art, sensation for judgement [a]nd it wants to impose that sensibility of undifferentiated experience upon all realms of culture' (RGE: 309). The combination of these two currents, one anti-aesthetic, the other anti-nomian, represents the greatest threat to the traditional role of the university as the repository and teacher of a great cultural tradition.

STUDENT PROTEST

In the early 1960s it appeared that planned change might be possible and indeed that the plans that were being best-laid were keeping American society on roughly the right track. It was an emerging post-industrial society that needed numerous scientists and technologists and the education system was gearing up to produce batches of numerate, hard-working, committed 'new men' (RGE: 86).[4] These schemes did in fact 'gang a-gley' quite early. In the late 1960s and early 1970s the newly educated 'baby boomer' generation of students tried to exercise its power in a series of active, occasionally violent, demonstrations and protests. Bell (CSRU; 1970) discusses these short-term and unpredictable changes as part of an attempt to understand the crisis of legitimacy in the universities marked by the student protests. He isolates five central factors contributing to this crisis of legitimacy (1970: 55–60). Not all of these had been forecast in RGE.[5] They were:

- *The Vietnam War*. The faltering American participation on the side of a pro-capitalist, authoritarian government against indigenous, nationalist-communist rebels raised deep questions about both the credibility and morality of the external extension of national military power. In particular, it raised questions about the contribution of American universities to defence research and intelligence-gathering.
- *Blacks*. The period saw the public emergence of an Afro-American identity. Bell argues that blacks were in an expressive, second-generation phase of aggressive hostility to the oppressor and they formed an increasing proportion of student numbers.
- *Multiplication of social problems*. Here Bell argues that the creation of a national society, its numerical expansion and the recognition of industrial side-effects such as pollution raised both the number and the visibility of social problems. All of these were beyond the wit of government to resolve: it did not know how to organize a welfare-delivery system; it could not realize its promises and visions because of its fractious and interest-bound legislature; and it could not legitimize taxation levels to support its programmes. These failures contributed to student disillusionment with government.
- *Post-industrial society*. The post-industrial society carries its own problems, argues Bell, because it creates its own structures of privilege, based on knowledge. Student protests were for Bell 'the early class struggles of the post-industrial society' in which the subordinate class was rebelling against the strictures

of educational rationalities that were increasing in post-industrialized mass education.
* *The new sensibility.* Modern elite culture is anti-institutional
  and anti-nomian (see Chapter 7 for a discussion of Bell's theoretical argument in support of this view) – it celebrates the
  individual as opposed to the social. However, modern artistic
  and intellectual expression always took a particular form by
  expressing, syncretizing or reacting against particular styles.
  The new sensibility, what some have called a postmodern sensibility, involved a rejection of form in favour of a celebration
  of experience and opinion. Bell interprets this as anti-intellectualism so that: 'Education becomes not the transmission of
  learning but a search for "meaningful identity" to be gained
  by "dialogue," "encounter," and "confrontation." ' (1970: 60)
  Certainly, it undermines the authoritative status of the teacher.

The background to the sources of student protest in the late
1960s and early 1970s is given in the above discussion: the rise
of mass higher education that concentrates large numbers of each
generation and constitutes academics as an occupational class;
the growth of research that devalues teaching; the rapid specialization of subfields that destroys academic communities; the politicization of universities by virtue of their involvement in
government service; and the refocusing of academic attention in a
cosmopolitan direction (CSRU: vii-ix). Bell and Kristol (CSRU:
ix-x) single out four, more proximate factors in the outburst of
student resentment: the 'organizational harness' of grade-chasing
and career commitment; the neglect of undergraduates by
research-orientated academics; the Vietnam war, a single event
that convinced many students of the deceit and incompetence of
governments and of their 'lackeys' in the universities; and the
failure of liberal politics to solve major social problems.

The combination of these factors led student protest into a
configuration that cannot be assimilated to traditional political
action. Although there was an original concern with the specific
issues of Vietnam, civil rights or the authoritarianism and traditionalism of universities, that concern, 'has been overwhelmed
by an onrush of anger, rancor, and a generational rage born of
seeming impotence' (CSRU: x). The style of student protest was
an attack on all forms of authority, moral order, discipline and
(self-)repression. Here it merged with the postmodern sensibility
and thus was legitimized by a prevailing moral culture that

emphasized expression of the self. Bell and Kristol capture the essence of the style in the term 'confrontation', a configuration in which political action is constituted as a symbolic gesture that can mobilize collective resentment and keep it alive by making the impossible demand for a 'total resolution' (CSRU: x-xi). Confrontational protests take on the features of a 'happening' or drama in which the means become ends in themselves because they have the effect of disempowering authority. Bell and Kristol differentiate general student protests that have this negative goal from militant black action that had the positive goal of equal social participation, a bid for status and power. They warn blacks that their involvement in the 'grotesque' expressionism of the confrontation might lead to the destruction of that vehicle that might carry them towards their goal, i.e. the university system.

Bell's own piece in CSRU (67–107) is a historical narrative of and an attempt at an explanation of a violent confrontation at Columbia in 1968 between students led by the radical group *Students for a Democratic Society* (SDS) and the university administration. He asks how a small vanguard could energize and radicalize over 500 other students into disruption and violence and how an administration noted for its avuncular tolerance towards students could become repressive and authoritarian.

To answer the first he mobilizes his argument about the effectiveness of ideology as a mobilizing force because it can unleash passion (see Chapter 4). The student body was receptive because it was politically liberal, but liberalism had failed in solving both domestic social problems and to win the Vietnam war. SDS, falsely in Bell's view, saw the university as the microcosm of society and thus found a moral justification for wrecking it. The seizure of a building by militant black students broke the constraints on liberal students and allowed them to be fired up by the ideology of SDS. Their liberal commitments had been, 'codified, given a moral content, and ... an antagonistic stance ... that allows an individual, without further doubts about his premises, to make a whole series of related judgements about new circumstances' (CSRU: 97). Bell discusses this development as a conversion experience akin to religious conversion and also as a phenomenon of mass contagion. Importantly, the new ideological commitment received confirmation at the moral level because it received financial support from the New York literary establishment, and at the cognitive level because the students' intellectual premises were never challenged by the administration.

Indeed, the 'reality test' was provided by police action that confirmed the students' accusation of authoritarianism.

Bell answers the second question, that of how 'a community, asking special loyalty from its members, can sanction the clubbing of its students' (CSRU: 101) in terms of political inexperience. The leaders had no idea about the politics of social movements or of ideology. It failed to distinguish between the SDS vanguard, for whom by implication Bell might view repression as appropriate, and the other 500. The latter were, for Bell, not wreckers but people with inchoate but conceivably legitimate grievances. The administration played into SDS hands by allowing it to provoke a repression that could only be self-defeating. The university, Bell insists, is a moral community and not a political society. This means that neither confrontation nor repression is appropriate to it. The only way it can avoid both is to assert itself as a moral community, that is, by committing itself to the fullest level of democratic and collegial participation possible by its members.

For Bell, SDS action in confronting the university was an expression of its failure to have any effect on the society in general: 'The New Left has been forced to retreat more and more into the university and to resort to more grandiose dreams and more megalomaniacal visions' (CSRU: 106). However, by the time he published 'Quo Warranto?' in 1970 it was clear that the student protest movement had, more or less, done its dash. The war was settled, the SDS was in disarray, and American politics was beginning to adopt a more conservative tone. He could only specify what the remnants of the movement would leave to future student generations in three alternative orientations (1970: 60–1): urban guerillas, violent cadres active in the wider society; 'crazies,' small groups willing to engage in random acts of violence; and the alienated. This last, relatively large group of puzzled, angry and concerned students worries Bell the most because they hold the future of the university in their hands. The only way to bring these back into the university community is to reform it by offering students a choice of type of institution, including some that concentrate on diffuse scholarship, by divesting some of the more commercial and governmental research institutes into the private sector, by restricting campuses to a human scale, and by increasing participation (1970: 63–5).

CONCLUSION

The topic of education allows Bell to put to work many of the theoretical themes for which he has now become famous in a single context and to demonstrate their explanatory power. Three stand out: the way in which education becomes linked to central governmental activities and a key focus for policy; the post-industrialization of the knowledge sector; and the disjunction between the reifications of the techno-economic structure, as expressed in increasing technicization, and the diremption of authority promoted by postmodernist culture. The analysis allows Bell to remain 'a conservative in culture'. RGE in particular is a proposal for the continued teaching of the Western cultural canon in contradistinction to possibilities either for 'creative' and self-exploratory types of course or for the inclusion of the cultural expressions of the oppressed. Against calls for the introduction of 'cultural studies' that seek to de-ideologize texts by 'deconstructing' them and that regard all texts as being of equal worth, Bell stands firm in a commitment to teaching the great texts of white, male, Western culture as the components of human wisdom. Whether the teaching of such an agenda can equally meet Bell's declared commitment to liberality might be open to debate, because it clearly closes off some cognitive opportunities. Opponents of Bell would argue that to confine education to the canon is, *de facto*, doctrinaire.

Whatever value-position one takes in relation to this view, Bell's analysis of the directions being taken by the university have been more or less confirmed by events over the 30 or so years since he wrote it. They have moved more firmly in the direction of techno-economization so that academics and students equally are decreasingly regarded as autonomous subjects and increasingly as reified objects, as human resources or student units with uses and applications rather than as human beings with a subjective consciousness. This is manifested in the increasing importation of the full paraphernalia of social control from the business world into academic contexts: in mission statements and TQM; in the glorification of the research grant and the diremption of scholarship and teaching; and in the displacement of collegial judgement by quantified performativity. The humanities have returned but in a more 'politically correct' form than Bell would probably find acceptable; science prospers as it garners ever larger amounts of money and ever fewer students; while social science has become intellectually bankrupt, retreating into a trivializing positivism and yielding academic leadership to that most techno-economized and disintellectualized of endeavours, the business school.

6

The Post-industrial Society

Chapter 4 introduces the first of Bell's 'big ideas', the notion that ideology has been exhausted as a principle for the organization of political life. In this chapter we address perhaps the biggest of his ideas, the one that has become the most influential both inside sociology and in wider intellectual circles, the idea that society is becoming 'post-industrial'. The term 'post-industrial society' has become common conceptual currency because of Bell's construction of it, even where that construction is not acknowledged, much as the concept of 'charisma' is invoked without making reference to Weber. This alone is a tribute to the effectiveness of the conceptualization.

The term 'post-industrial society' is used to describe a series of contemporary macro-social changes. Bell had sensed that such changes were occurring as early as 1950. One of the historical shifts that was contributing to the decomposition of Marxist ideology was the reconstruction of the techno-economic structure. Bell gropes for a term to describe it:

> In the dimly-emerging social structure, new power sources are being created and new power sources are

being formed. Whatever the character of that new social structure may be – whether state capitalism, managerial society, or corporative capitalism – by 1950 American socialism as a political and social fact had become simply a notation in the archives of history. [MS: 193]

By the late 1950s he had the terminology within his grasp. In 1959 he gave lectures using the term 'post-Industrial society' at the Salzburg Seminar in Austria and in 1962 he wrote a long paper on the topic under the title 'The Post-Industrial Society: A Speculative View of the United States and Beyond'. This must be one of the most influential unpublished papers ever written because it circulated widely in academic and public policy circles. It was pirated both in *Current* and in *Dun's Review* and it moved the journal *Science* (12/6/64) to comment:

One of the prophets most honoured by quotation and imitation is Daniel Bell, Columbia University sociologist and a former labor editor of *Fortune* who drew a convincing and intimidating picture of what is coming, barring war, in a paper called "The Post-industrial Society". [in Bell 1971a: 167n]

Bell decided not to publish at the time, however, 'because I felt that the idea was unfinished' (1971: 167n). However, the temptations of public exposure could not be resisted for long and several papers incorporating the original idea appeared in the mid- to late 1960s. One such that must be close to original appeared in a volume on scientific progress (1967a) and a set of more developed 'notes' on the concept appeared in *The Public Interest* at about the same time (1967b; 1967c). The 'notes' had a widespread, international impact. The various essays that Bell wrote on the topic were collected and published as *The Coming of Post-Industrial Society: a Venture in Social Forecasting* (COPIS) in 1973.

Bell is hesitant about taking credit for the invention of the term. He developed it originally, self-consciously to debate Dahrendorf's claims about changes in the class structure of contemporary industrial society (1959). However, it had been used by Riesman in an essay called 'Leisure and Work in Post-industrial Society' published in 1958. Bell admits: 'I had, quite likely, read Riesman's essay at the time and the phrase undoubtedly came from him, though I have developed it in various writings in a vastly different way' (1971a: 167n). Certainly, Bell does not intend the term to mean a post-work society as Riesman did. In any event, the issue of terminological originality is redundant because it was first used by a now obscure British socialist theorist, Arthur Penty, as early as 1917 [COPIS: 37n].[1]

Curiously, Bell received little credit among his immediate contemporaries for his development of the idea. Kuhns' *The Post-industrial Prophets* (1971) does not include or even reference Bell. Kleinberg gives large coverage to Bell's end-of-ideology thesis and even makes reference to the 'notes', but for him the concept of 'post-industrial society' is evanescent, having 'become widely ad[o]pted as a basic term of reference for discussions of the new society' (1973: 1). Touraine's book entitled *The Post-industrial Society* (1971), originally published in French in 1969, makes no reference to Bell.[2]

Bell outlines four intellectual influences on the formulation (1971a: 165–7):

- his own analysis of the break-up of family capitalism in which he proposes that societies are no longer ruled by business managers but by a technical-intellectual elite (EI: 39–46; see Chapter 3) – 'the perennial interest of a sociologist in scanning the historical skies for a "new class" was the starting point of the argument' (1971a: 165–6);
- studies of the changing composition of the labour force done at *Fortune* that drew on Clark's classification of employment into three sectors (primary, secondary and tertiary) (1957) and a subsequent study by Foote and Hatt (1953) that extended the idea into quaternary and quinary sectors;
- a reading of Schumpeter (1942) that turned his mind to technological forecasting; and
- a paper by a historian of science, Gerald Holton (1962), that emphasized that the path of innovation in science was best reflected in the codifications of theory.

The post-industrial-society concept put these ideas, a new ruling elite, the movement of the labour force into service sectors, technology as the driving force of change and theory as the most important type of knowledge, into an entirely novel and challenging sociological account of changing social structure.

Before proceeding to an outline of the theory it needs to be located generally within the three-realms paradigm introduced in Chapter 2. Bell insists throughout his analysis, and against the understandings of many of his critics, that it is only the techno-economic realm of society, the realm that he often calls the 'social structure', that can become post-industrial. Social structure can become post-industrial regardless of political regime or cultural configuration. Indeed, he goes further in distinguishing two dimensions *within* social structure, the socio-economic (patterns of economic ownership) and the socio-technical (see Figure 1, p. xx), and it is only in the second of these that the transition to post-industrialism can occur (COPIS: ix-xii). The issue of whether a society is post-industrial is therefore not only independent of whether it is Christian or Islamic, democratic or totalitarian, but also of whether it is capitalist or socialist. Indeed, if these dimensions are truly autonomous, one might presumably encounter a feudal post-industrial society or even a tribal post-industrial society (although Bell does not admit to either of these possibilities). The line Bell takes is not only an attack on the holistic and deterministic theories to which he is opposed, but also serves to defend him against critics who accuse him of constructing a convergence thesis.

THE CONCEPTUAL PRISM

The 'post-industrial society', then, is a theory of social change. It argues that contemporary societies are or will be going through a shift so that the post-industrial society that emerges will be as different from industrial society as industrial society is from pre-industrial society. We can perhaps begin by considering the distinctions that Bell makes between these three (COPIS: 116–19, 126–9). It must be remembered that Bell intends this distinction only to be analytic, which, in his terms, means that while societies may appear different when viewed through this particular 'prism' or typology they may be similar when viewed through another. Also, Bell does not argue that one type displaces the preceding one but that rather: 'Like palimpsests, the new developments overlie the previous layers, erasing some features and thickening the texture of society as a whole.' (COPIS: xvi)

A *pre-industrial society* can be characterized as 'a game against nature' that centres on attempts to extract resources from the natural environment. Primary-sector occupations and industries (hunting, foraging, farming, fishing, mining, forestry) dominate its economy. Economic activity is carried out according to custom and tradition and faces severe limitations from the supply of land and resources. The level of economic activity varies according to the seasons and to global fluctuations in demand. The possession of land determines the pattern of stratification. The unit of social life is the extended household which, above the level of manual labour, often includes a relatively large number of domestic servants.

An *industrial society* is a 'a game against fabricated nature' that centres on human-machine relationships and applies energy to the transformation of the natural into a technical environment. Economic activity focuses on the manufacturing and processing of tangible goods. The central occupations are the secondary sector ones of semi-skilled factory worker and engineer.[3] The chief economic problem is the mobilization of sufficient capital to establish manufacturing enterprises. By contrast, the main social problem is located in the stratification system. That system depends on the differential ownership of capital and is likely to give rise to industrial or class conflict about the distribution of returns to capital and labour. So another key problem is the co-ordination of differentiated activities and interests around machine technology.

By contrast, a *post-industrial society* is 'a "game between persons" in which an "intellectual technology," based on information, rises alongside of machine technology' (COPIS: 116).[4] The post-industrial society involves industries from three sectors: the tertiary industries of transportation and utilities; the quaternary industries of trade, finance and capital exchange; and the quinary industries of health, education, research, public administration and leisure. Among these, the last is definitive because the key occupations are the professional and technical ones, with scientists at the core. Given that the generation of information is the key problem and that science is the most important source of information, the organization of the institutions of science, the universities and research institutes is the central problem in the post-industrial society. The strength of nations is given in their scientific capacity and: 'For this reason the nature and kinds of state support for science, the politicization of science, the socio-logical problems of the organization of work by science teams, all become central policy issues in a post-industrial society' (COPIS: 117–18).

Bell elaborates his ideal-typical construct of the post-indus-trial society in terms of five dimensions, a methodology that presumably emulates Weber's dimensions of the ideal type of bureaucratic administrative staff. They are as follows (COPIS: 14–33):

- *Creation of a service economy.* Here Bell conceptualizes social change in terms of what Miles and Gershuny (1986) call 'a march through the sectors'. As discussed in Chapter 2, the techno-economic structure of a society changes according to an economizing principle in which more efficient and productive techniques and production systems replace less efficient and productive ones. Drawing on Clark (1957), Bell argues that change therefore involves unilinear progression between the sectors (primary through quinary) and a corresponding shift in the labour force. Accordingly: 'the first and simplest character- istic of a post-industrial society is that the majority of the labor force is no longer engaged in agriculture or manufacturing but in services, which are defined, residually, as trade, finance, transport, health, recreation, research, education, and govern- ment' (COPIS: 15). On this criterion the USA had the first service economy by the mid-1950s but it has now been joined by much of the Western world, Japan and some of the Asian dragons. Bell cautions about the particular use that he gives to the word 'services' (against misreadings by such critics as Kumar 1978: 242ff). He intends it to apply not to personal and manual services but only those found in health, education, research and public administration.

- *The pre-eminence of the professional and technical class.* Here Bell tells us that the predominant, although not necessarily the majority of, occupations in the society will be professional and technical occupations requiring a tertiary level of education. The core will be scientists and engineers and together they will become a knowledge class that displaces the propertied bourgeoisie.[5]

- *The primacy of theoretical knowledge.* This is the defining 'axial principle' of the post-industrial society, the organization of the society around knowledge that becomes the basis for social control, the direction of innovation and the political manage- ment of new social relationships. Bell stresses that in a post- industrial society this knowledge is theoretical, rather than traditional or practical, in character. It involves the codification of knowledge into abstract symbolic systems that can be applied in a wide variety of situations. The scientist displaces the inventor; the econometrician displaces the political economist.

- *The planning of technology.* The advance of theoretical knowledge allows technological forecasting, that is, the planning of change, including forward assessments of its risks, costs and advantages.[6] The control and regulation of the future introduction of technologies becomes feasible.
- *The rise of a new intellectual technology.* Against usual understandings of technology as physical, as to do with tools or machines, Bell introduces the idea of an intellectual technology, a system of abstract symbols that can model those 'games between people' and allow one to make decisions without intuition: 'An intellectual technology is the substitution of algorithms (problem-solving rules) for intuitive judgements' (COPIS: 29). The computer is a physical technology that is necessary to this development because only by the use of a computer can the multiple complexities involved be calculated. However the critical intellectual technology is the software and the statistical or logical formulae that are entered into the computer.

In a foreword written for a new edition of COPIS published in 1978 Bell alters this list of dimensions. The planning dimension is eliminated and seven new dimensions are added. These are (COPIS: xvi-xix):

- *A change in the character of work.* Work focuses not on the manipulation of objects but on an engagement in relationships with other people.
- *The role of women.* The expansion of the services sector provides a basis for the economic independence of women that had not previously been available.[7]
- *Science as the imago.* Scientific institutions and their relationship with other institutions are the central, emergent and 'perfect' feature of the post-industrial society.
- *Situses as political units.* A situs is defined as a vertical order of a society, as opposed to the horizontal orders of classes or strata. Bell specifies four functional situses (scientific, technological, administrative and cultural) and five institutional situses (business, government, university/research, social welfare and military). Major conflicts will occur between situses rather than between classes and, indeed, class formation may well be prevented.

- *Meritocracy.* Position is allocated on the basis of education and skill rather than wealth or cultural advantage.
- *The end of scarcity?* Scarcity of goods will disappear in favour of scarcities of information and time. A key problem may be the allocation of leisure time.
- *The economics of information.* Because information is essentially a collective rather than a private good, it will be necessary to follow a co-operative, rather than an individualistic strategy in the generation and use of information (perhaps the creation of a 'public household' – see Chapter 4).

The dimensions are now multiplying like rabbits and Bell seeks to bring us back to the core of his proposal by specifying that there are two 'large' dimensions by which one decides whether a social structure has yet entered a post-industrial phase. These are, the centrality of theoretical knowledge (including by implication, the employment of science as a means to technological change) and the expansion of the quinary service sector. We can now move on to examine the consequences of these two shifts in some detail.

A SERVICE SOCIETY

Bell disentangles the move towards a service economy into several components (COPIS: 127–9). First, industrial society itself presupposes an expansion of certain 'manual' service industries, transportation, communication, public utilities and wholesale and retail distribution. Second, white-collar employment grows in the 'co-ordinating' sectors of the economy, banking and finance. Third, as goods production begins to exceed immediate needs and as individual incomes rise, personal and leisure services (grooming, dining, leisure travel, entertainment, sport, etc.) expand. Fourth, the conception of rights to health and education expands. Last, the increasing complexity of society and the increasing politicization of rights and entitlements leads to an expansion of public-sector services.

In so far as the USA is the emerging post-industrial society, Bell (COPIS: 129–33) can now move on to examine the march through the sectors in that society. The overall picture confirms the existence of such a trend: in 1900 30 per cent of American workers were employed in service-sector industries (tertiary, quaternary, quinary); in 1940 50 per cent were so employed; and by

1980 the proportion had reached 70 per cent. Until 1920 this development was the consequence of declining agricultural employment and service employment grew only in the tertiary sector. Thereafter, the share of secondary sector employment itself began to shrink, even though its absolute numbers increased. After 1947 the most important area of service employment growth was government, so that by 1980 it accounted for about 16 per cent of the labour force although a major component of this was the expansion in the area of education. Bell is also acutely aware that sectoral distribution does not necessarily inform us about the distribution of manual vs. non-manual labour. Many employees in the service sector are manual workers and about one-third of the manufacturing employees are non-manual. He forecasts that not only will the secondary-sector share of employment decline but that the proportion of manual workers in manufacturing will also decline as automation takes hold.

This leads Bell (COPIS: 134–7) into an analysis of the occupational distribution of the American labour force. The proportion of the labour force in white-collar (excluding personal service) occupations rose from 17 per cent in 1900 to 50 per cent in 1980. He admits that much of this change has been due to the absorption of women into routine white-collar employment. However, even if one looks solely at male employment the transformation has been remarkable; the share in white-collar occupations increased from 15 to 42 per cent between 1900 and 1970. By comparison, blue-collar (manual-industrial) occupations peaked at about 40 per cent in 1940 before declining to 32 per cent in 1980; and agricultural employment slid from 37 per cent in 1900 to 2 per cent in 1980. A key element in Bell's argument is that the fastest-growing occupational group of all is the professional and technical group. It was less than a million in 1890 and now numbers over 12 million, or 16 per cent of the labour force. Four million of these are teachers and health workers but 2.3 million are in science and engineering.

This development poses severe difficulties for the trade union movement which Bell clearly regards as a phenomenon of industrial society (COPIS: 137–42). American union membership advanced rapidly between 1935 and 1947 but since then the level of union density has declined from 30 to 27 per cent in 1980.[8] This slight shift masks some considerable internal redistributions of membership. The causes of the reduction lie in declining blue-collar employment (where unionization continues to stand at about 60 per cent) and in rising female employment. The only real area of union growth is in the area of government employment, but private-sector, white-collar employment is a difficult arena of recruitment. Financial service employees remain largely unorganized.

Bell can now examine some of the issues that arise from the emergence of a service labour force and that differentiate it from an industrial labour force. He discusses five such issues, focusing on their implications for social division and conflict:

- *Education and status* (COPIS: 143–5) The 'post-industrial labour force is highly educated and, in so far as it is decreasingly fed by migration, culturally homogeneous. This allows Bell to ask whether this might provide the basis for the emergence of a new proletarian consciousness of a type envisioned by Marx, but he remains agnostic on the issue. Indeed, he is agnostic on the exact form of labour organization that new professional employees will set up.
- *Blacks* (COPIS: 145) Bell recalls that in his first specification of the post-industrial-society concept in 1962 he had suggested that class would disappear in favour of a system of social inequality based primarily on race. In 1973 he sees little reason to change his mind, although the stress of post-industrial occupations on performance criteria has provided a slightly increased measure of equality.
- *Women* (COPIS: 146) The service economy is highly feminized. About half the workers in the services sector are women, compared with 20 per cent of employees in the goods-producing sectors. Women employees present a particular recruitment problem for organized labour that historically has excluded them.
- *The non-profit sector* (COPIS: 146–7) The non-profit sector of the service economy is growing much faster than the private sector. Indeed, it is the major area for the net growth of new jobs, so that by 1980 about 20 per cent of the labour force was in non-profit-sector jobs. In so far as many of these workers are middle class they will have both an increased appetite for cultural products and a more liberal set of social and political attitudes.
- *The 'new' working class* (COPIS: 148–54) The educated and professionalized sections of the working class are unlikely to become a militant and radicalized vanguard for the rest of the

(disappearing) proletariat. Rather, they are likely to be drawn into the system of professional situses which is a more likely possibility for socio-economic conflict.

Bell sums up the character of the emerging service economy in the following passage:

> [W]hat is central to the new relationship is encounter or communication, and the response of ego to alter, and back – from the irritation of a customer at an airline-ticket office to the sympathetic or harassed response of teacher and student. But the fact that individuals now talk to other individuals rather than interact with a machine, is the fundamental fact about work in the post-industrial society. [COPIS: 163]

For Bell, this means profound implications for the central conflicts and divisions in society. He recognizes the possibility that particular events, such as foreign competition, may occasionally heighten labour militancy but, in a return to an earlier theme, he thinks it unlikely that this will constitute ideologically organized class warfare. Politics is likely to focus on what he calls communal issues – health, education, the environment and crime – on which labour may often be divided or, indeed, allied with capital.

A KNOWLEDGE SOCIETY

We can now turn to the second 'large dimension' of the post-industrial society, the centrality of theoretical knowledge and the institutions of science. In an unusual step Bell gives a formal definition of knowledge, 'a set of organized statements of facts or ideas, presenting a reasoned judgement or an experimental result, which is transmitted to others through some communication medium in some systematic form' (COPIS: 175; italics deleted). However, because he proposes to measure the growth of knowledge, he needs an operational rather than a formal definition, which he also offers: 'Knowledge is that which is objectively known, an intellectual property, attached to a name or group of names and certified by copyright or some other form of social recognition (e.g. publication)' (COPIS: 176). He insists that such knowledge is social, as opposed to individual, in terms of both its production and cost and in terms of its evaluation by the market.

Bell more or less accepts a formulation from Price that the rate of growth of scientific papers and of books has always been exponential rather than lineal, with a doubling time of about fifteen years. However, growth in any field of science always hits limits[9] and outputs of knowledge actually increase as the consequence of the differentiation or 'branching' of science, 'the creation of new and numerous subdivisions or specialties within fields' (COPIS: 186). This happens continuously: in 1948 the *National Register of Scientific and Technical Personnel* listed 54 scientific specializations; by 1968 there were 900.

Technology has grown equally rapidly. Bell surveys several estimates of the rate of technological change, measured largely by general increases in productivity (average output per worker). Productivity typically increases by roughly 2 per cent per year, give or take 0.5 per cent. Before the Second World War it was usually below 2 per cent, and after that war it was usually above 2 per cent (COPIS: 189–95). However, Bell claims that in the post-industrial society something radically new is occurring in the area of technology, 'the changed relationship between science and technology, and the incorporation of science through the institutionalization of research into the ongoing structure of the economy... as a normal part of business organization' (COPIS: 196). Research is becoming organized systematically rather than operating on a piecemeal basis and industries are becoming more science-based. Productivity is therefore likely to escalate.

Taking these developments together Bell argues that the post-industrial society is a knowledge society. In a knowledge society science and technology become intimately related because technology is driven by theoretical as opposed to practical knowledge; and the shares of employment of GDP in the knowledge field become relatively large (COPIS: 212). Bell seeks to show that the USA is moving into just such a configuration. For example, the proportion of GDP devoted to education doubled from 3.5 to 7.5 per cent between 1949 and 1969 (COPIS: 216–20).[10] More impressively, the proportion of GNP devoted to research and development multiplied fifteen times between 1948 and 1965 to reach 3 per cent. Most of this funding came from government, so that a large proportion was committed to defence and atomic energy research. However, almost all of the rest went into physical and medical sciences. Spending in these areas is growing much faster than in defence and atomic energy research (COPIS: 250–62).

The development of a knowledge society incorporates 'a democratization of higher education on a scale that the world has never seen before'. The proportion of 18–21-year-olds enrolled in education doubled between 1946 and 1964 to 44 per cent. The average doubling time for the American university population is 20 years (since 1879), but since the Second World War the rate of increase accelerated rapidly by virtue of enrolments in graduate degrees. So by 1970 the doubling time had come down to ten years. Importantly, while only about a quarter of first degrees are in science, more than half the doctorates are in natural science and mathematics (COPIS: 216–20).

From a sociological point of view, Bell makes a more important claim that those who work in the knowledge sectors come to constitute a 'knowledge class'. The members are some of those he has already discussed in his analysis of the service economy – teachers, engineers, technicians and scientists. The last is the most 'crucial group'. Whereas the work-force increased by 50 per cent between 1930 and 1975, and the number of engineers increased by 370 per cent, the number of scientists increased by 930 per cent (475,000). In 1970 the 'scientific population' was about four million or 4.7 per cent of the work-force (COPIS: 216–17).

Bell works through a conceptual filtering process to identify the scientific elite, the equivalent of the capitalist bourgeoisie, by progressively eliminating teachers, those without doctorates and those not engaged in research. The resulting select group of perhaps 120,000 scientific and technical personnel is very different from the population as a whole in so far as less than a quarter are employed in (industrial) business and more than a half in universities. Here he shows that he really does mean that this elite is a knowledge *class*:

> If one believes ... that the expansion of science and scientifically based technology is creating the framework for a new social order that will erode capitalism, as the activities of the merchants and the bourgeois outside the landed economy undermined feudalism, then the significant fact is that most of the activities of science are outside the business system and the organization of science policy is not, in the first instance, responsive to business demand. The necessary foundation for any new

> class is to have an independent institutional base outside
> the old dominant order. For the scientist this base has
> been the university. [COPIS: 232]

While Bell is in no doubt that scientists constitute a new class he remains uncertain about whether they can maintain sufficient independence ever to undermine capitalism.

It follows though that the university is a critical institution. Certainly, current rates of expansion might give Bell cause to believe that an institutional base for the knowledge class will continue to be available. More importantly, he is able to isolate a smallish group of largish universities, perhaps 100 or 150 of the 2,500 in the USA, that teach most of the undergraduates and do nearly all the graduate teaching and research. Indeed, twenty-one such universities carried out 54 per cent of the research. It is critical to the pre-eminence of the knowledge class that this core should maintain the relatively high level of autonomy that derives from private sources of funding, and Bell sees a threat to such autonomy in the declining share of enrolment received by the major private universities (Harvard, Stanford, etc.)

A COMMUNAL SOCIETY

Bell's claims about the rise of a knowledge class appear problematic to many sociologists. The argument that social inequality might be based on the intangibles of theory and information rather than on the solidities of material property or even occupation runs counter to a century of sociological tradition.

In a nutshell, Bell's stratification claim is twofold: first, that the basis of stratification in the post-industrial society will shift from property to knowledge, and thus from class to status, so that the knowledge 'class' becomes the most powerful status-group in society; and second, that there will be intersecting dimensions of inequality such that no particular cleavage can be regarded as fundamental.[11] Society will come to approximate a community not merely because inequalities cross-cut but because the form of decision-making changes as social structures enter the post-industrial phase. Industrial society is organized as a market in which the intersection of multiple individual choices determines outcomes, but the post-industrial society requires social decisions, that is, consensus on planning future developments. However, as the discussion of Bell's concept of the public household in the preceding chapters indicates, consensus is extraordinarily difficult to achieve in the context of an escalation of claims and entitlements. A conflict between populist claims and professional expertise is a real possibility. So the post-industrial society need not be communal in the sense that it realizes a utopian harmony:

> If the struggle between capitalist and worker, in the locus of the factory, was the hallmark of industrial society, the clash between the professional and the populace, in the organization and in the community is the hallmark of conflict in the post-industrial society. [COPIS: 129]

Rather, it is a community only in so far as many of its decisions need to be made by collectivized groups.

We can now examine these claims in more detail. At the gross level of the ideal type, the sources of power and who wields it are quite clear. In an industrial society the key issue is control of capital plant and machinery and it is the business class that controls these, exercising political power through indirect influence on governmental decisions and reproducing itself through direct inheritance, patronage and educational inheritance. In a post-industrial society the key resource is knowledge and this is under the control of scientists and researchers influencing political processes by being engaged and incorporated in governmental decisions and reproducing itself largely through education (COPIS: 359). However, because contemporary social structure is not completely post-industrial it combines a mixture of power and mobility mechanisms including wealth and property, political position and credentialized skill. Nevertheless, two features of this complex confirm a shift in the power structure: the common interest of the scientific elite in promoting professional or ethical rather than material outcomes; and the reconstitution of individual and private property into organizational property. (COPIS: 360–2)

These developments do not imply that politics will become less important but rather the reverse. The reasons are that: society must be organized on a national rather than a regional or local basis if planning and co-ordination are to prove effective; and multiplying claims for entitlements are made through politics. Decisions about planning and entitlements cannot be made simply on the basis of technical rationality but imply political value-judgements (COPIS: 364). Politics therefore becomes the 'cockpit' of the post-industrial society, the visible hand that co-ordinates where the market no longer can be effective. Its activities have been enlarged and problematized by five developments[12] (COPIS: 468–71):

- the openness of government has increased and avenues for access have multiplied;
- telecommunications have increased the frequency of interaction between the members of society;
- families are more mobile and more technologized so their members engage in more frequent exchanges with others;
- there is an increased need for planning; and
- advancing levels of consumption make imperative an increased regulation of competition between individuals and groups for resources.

It follows from this that:

> In terms of status (esteem and recognition, and possibly income) the knowledge class may be the highest class in the new society, but there is no intrinsic reason [that it should] become a new economic interest class, or a new political class which would bid for power. [COPIS: 374–5]

Bell's overall scheme for the 'societal structure' of the post-industrial society therefore includes three dimensions that are somewhat reminiscent of Weber's class-status-party triplet. These are status, situs and control, although in Bell they are all dimensions of 'the classes'. Status is the 'horizontal' dimension that sets up the knowledge strata. There are four such strata: the professional class, technicians and semi-professionals, clerical and sales workers, and craftsmen and semi-skilled workers. In a mix-and-match of stratification terminology, the professional 'class' is subdivided into four 'estates': scientific, that develops basic knowledge and is autonomous; technical, that applies knowledge to practical problems; administrative that manages organizations; and cultural, that is involved with the expressive symbolization of forms and meanings. Conflict is possible between these estates on the basis of ethical differences: e.g. between a professional ethos and an ethos of self-interest; or between a rational ethos and an expressive ethos (COPIS: 375–6).

Bell uses the term 'situs' to indicate the 'vertical' structures of society that are 'the actual locuses of occupational activities and interests'. There are five: economic enterprises; government;

universities and research institutes; social service organizations; and the military. A peculiar feature of the post-industrial society is that statuses are not concentrated within situses but are scattered across them. In an industrial society, capital and labour are defined by the economic situs alone, but scientists in a post-industrial society can be found in any situs.

As the preceding discussion indicates, a new feature of post-industrial society is the importance of government. Whereas, in previous configurations, distributional disputes were fought out between capital and labour in the economic enterprise they are now being fought out within the 'control system' between an expanded number of interest groups that are frequently situs-based. The control system is broadly divided between a 'directorate' of senior government officials and 'the polities' including parties, non-governmental elites, interest and lobby groups, and mobilized claimants (COPIS: 375–7).

CONCLUSION

One of the reasons that Weber's work has had a particularly seminal effect is that, although he often engages in a tedious semanticism, his work is also often loose and incomplete as well as being extraordinarily suggestive and insightful. Neo-Weberians can spend many happy hours, indeed whole careers, of scholarship chasing down alternative possible conceptualizations and typological arrangements. Bell offers those who study him similar opportunities and nowhere is this more true than in the case of the post-industrial society. To be frank, the concept is slippery, not through any attempt at dissimulation but rather because the essayistic style that Bell adopts encourages expressiveness at the possible expense of analytic precision.

Analytic imprecision is not difficult to find. The very term 'post-industrial society' is imprecise because Bell frequently insists that he is not arguing about all three realms of society but only about the techno-economic or social structure. The polity and the culture are supposed to turn through their own cycles in blissful isolation. Even so, Bell cannot resist telling us that the form of the polity will be communal in the post-industrial society. Equally we cannot be entirely clear about his methodology. Perhaps the clearest statement of intent is on the first page of the 1978 Foreword, where he says that it is a speculative construct that identifies emergent features against which future reality can be measured. But there is an awful lot of straightforward narrative and description in the book that has little to do with ideal types or prisms and a lot to do with the peculiarities of American social development. Another inconsistency surrounds the discussion of axial principles and structures. In the three-realms argument (published in full after COPIS), the axial principle of the TES is economizing and its axial structure is bureaucracy. However, bureaucracy loses top billing in COPIS to the collegial structures of the university and the axial principle is variously specified as 'intellectual technology' (COPIS: ix), 'the centrality of theoretical knowledge' (COPIS: 115) or both (COPIS: 212). We can easily find other inconsistencies, about whether the post-industrial society has actually arrived or is merely a typological construct, and, if it has arrived, when it began, or about the usage of such terms as 'class', 'status' and 'polity', but this would be fruitless because the importance of the book lies in its capacity to sensitize us to a significant social shift rather than in laying out an analytical grid.

This sort of quibbling is common in relation to Bell and in relation to this book in particular and frequently tempts somewhat uncharitable responses (see e.g. Archer 1990; Kumar 1978; Miller 1975; Pahl 1975). If we are to criticize we might more profitably concentrate on whatever theoretical weakness there is in the argument. These seem to be twofold. First, as Nichols (1975: 350) has it, Bell by assertion shuts tight all the doors on any claim that he is theorizing an end to capitalism and class, especially in so far as he claims that technology is on a different dimension from property ownership. However, throughout the book, and particularly in the sections on stratification, it is clear that, in Bell's view, neither society as a whole nor the TES alone will be structured by capital accumulation in the future. This formulation surely must be a designed to deny the reality of business power in a claim that is perhaps a little too anti-Marxist. Second, and to return to a criticism raised in the preceding chapter, Bell forecasts the development of an enlarged communal state as if it can only happen in some future society. In fact, liberal corporatist states have long existed elsewhere than in the USA that have frequently successfully managed to balance claims within a reasoned political philosophy. The underdevelopment of the state has been both the poverty and the strength of American society, but it should not be taken to be a general feature of all advanced societies.

Notwithstanding these qualifications, the force of much of the argument cannot be denied. As Bell himself says, almost with surprise, the phrase 'post-industrial society' has passed quickly into the sociological literature (COPIS: ix).[13] The argument must be regarded as strongest in its stress on the emergence of the quinary service sector and the development of information as a resource, and perhaps weakest in its claims for a scientocracy and the centrality of universities. Certainly, few scientists would see themselves as members of a dominant or even rising social group, and universities twist and turn in the winds of governmental and private-sector funding flows. These strengths and weaknesses are perhaps reflected in the ways in which sociologists conventionally use the term. Every sociologist knows that 'post-industrialization' means the displacement of manufacturing occupations by service occupations, and indeed the description of such jobs as 'post-industrial occupations' is common parlance.

7

The Contradictions of Culture

Bell interprets the first two of his 'big ideas' in value-positive terms. He greets the end of ideology with a sigh of relief and the coming of post-industrial society with an unabashed and almost breathless enthusiasm. However, his interpretation of the third, the idea that contemporary culture is riven by irresolvable contradictions (CCC; 1990a), is quite clearly value-negative. In line with his proud admission that he is a conservative relative to culture, Bell is shocked and horrified by its chaotic and, to use one his favourite words, antinomian character. Contemporary culture carries no weight of authority, neither political nor moral, but is merely opinionistic, faddish and self-indulgent. For Bell, a culture needs to provide its adherents with a clear sense of what is ethical, what is aesthetic and what is factual (CCC: xv). Culture should have the canonical flavour of a transcendent religion that provides a common set of standards rather than the voluntaristic character of a bazaar where the only standard of consumption is gratification. The postmodernist cultural path in particular is for Bell a collectively nihilistic development.

Bell's main statements on culture are to be found in a collection of essays first published in 1976 (CCC) not long after the publication of COPIS. A noteworthy feature of the collection is that it appears to contradict the general tenor of the earlier one. In COPIS Bell predicts a rosy future in which an advancing technology will progressively liberate people from the drudgery of industrial work, in which society will be ruled by an enlightened scientific elite and in which a new societal community appears to be a genuine possibility. CCC, by contrast, speaks to rampant consumerism and self-indulgence, the diremption of artistic and moral standards and the disintegration of value-systems. The two appear to be irreconcilable, but for Bell, it must be remembered, such a reconciliation is unnecessary. The realms of TES and culture follow their own independent paths and the precise point that Bell wants to make is that there are contradictions between the drive for efficiency in the TES and the drive for self-realization in modern culture. As Bell puts it, CCC 'stands in a dialectical relation' to COPIS (CCC: xxx), the argument between the volumes representing the contradiction in society. However, a curious consequence has been a marked difference in the reception given to the two books. COPIS is regarded with deep suspicion in critical sociological circles because of its apparent technological determinism and its linear developmental claims, but it achieved wide public recognition, especially among the lay educated groups that are often mentioned in the publicity blurbs of book publishers. Possibly because it is so critical of the cultural implications of contemporary capitalism, CCC appeals to many academics engaged in cultural theory and indeed Bell is often nominated in a pantheon that includes such unlikely comrades as Michel Foucault, Fredric Jameson and Jean Baudrillard. However, it would probably be fair to say that Bell's cultural writings have not achieved the widespread public influence of those of say Edward Said, Robert Hughes or Allan Bloom.

Yet culture is possibly the most important of the realms in Bell's sociology. Culture is the site of an altered effectivity in the pattern of social change. For most of the history of Western industrial society, change originated in the TES where capitalism wrought population shifts, imposed work and time disciplines and diverted appropriated surplus into accumulative ventures. Culture remained undisturbed and separate: the aesthetic and the cognitive were locked away in the museum and the university; and the ethical was confined to the private sphere of family and church. However, during the middle fifty years of the twentieth century, 'the culture has taken the initiative in promoting change, and the economy has been geared to meeting these new wants' (CCC: xxv; italics deleted). Bell gives two reasons why culture has become supreme, why, 'what is played out in the imagination of the artist foreshadows, however dimly, the social reality of tomorrow' (CCC: 33). First, art has itself reflexively fixated on change and novelty so that rather than seeking to reproduce tradition it constantly seeks innovative forms and sensations. Second, society now regards culture not as a source of authoritative morality but precisely as a producer of new and titillating sensations. Therefore, 'our culture has an unprecedented mission: it is an official, ceaseless search for a new sensibility' (CCC: 34).

Two institutional changes reflect this development: first the avant-garde has been institutionalized so that art can no longer shock a society that is itself shocking; and second, society and art have come together in the market so that aesthetic aura and conceptions of high culture have disappeared. The sources of innovation in contemporary culture are therefore the fantastic possibilities created by mass media that, by definition, operate in the public sphere: 'The media are geared to feeding new images to people, to unsettling traditional conventions, and to the highlighting of aberrant and quirky behavior which becomes imagos for others to imitate' (CCC: xxv-xxvi). By contrast, Bell argues, the constraints of bureaucratism and trade unionism render economic enterprises highly resistant to change.[1]

The autonomization of culture, Bell argues, presents problems for the discipline of sociology (CCC: 37–8). Sociological practice was institutionalized on the claim that it could predict behaviour, attitudes and interests stochastically on the basis of such attributes of social location as age, gender, class and religion. For an increasing proportion of the population this is no longer true. Lifestyle, value-choice and aesthetic preference have become more idiosyncratic and personal. The source is not merely the expansion of discretionary income that provides for expanded patterns of consumption but the levelling and declassing effect of the expansion of education that has in turn widened the scope of what Bell now calls 'discretionary social behaviour'. If it is true then, that culture is where the sociological action now lies, then Bell's analysis of culture might be a more significant contribution than his more famous analysis of the post-industrial society.

CULTURE

Bell offers several different definitions of culture, of which a more or less ostensive one is quoted on p. 34 of this book. Perhaps his fullest and most revealing definition is the following:

> Culture, for a society, a group, or a person, is a continual process of sustaining an identity through the coherence gained by a consistent aesthetic point of view, a moral conception of self, and a style of life which exhibits those conceptions in the objects that adorn one's home and oneself and in the taste which expresses those points of view. Culture is thus the realm of sensibility, of emotion and moral temper, and of the intelligence, which seeks to order these feelings. [CCC: 36]

Two features of this definition are noteworthy. First, it is a traditional or conservative definition: the aesthetic point of view must be 'consistent'; the conception of self must be 'moral'; and feelings and emotions must be ordered intelligently rather than given free rein. This will give Bell problems in theorizing the contemporary set of amoral, transitory and hedonistic preferences that under this definition cannot be regarded as a culture. Second, it is a highly personalized definition (i.e. focused on 'oneself') in which the individual is subordinated to a shared or collective definition of appropriate behaviour and taste.

A key dimension of culture is its degree of unification with social structure. Against the three-realms argument outlined in Chapter 3, Bell suggests that 'most cultures and social structures have exhibited unity' (CCC: 36) despite the occasional instance of deviance: classical culture was united in the pursuit of virtue; medieval Christian culture was unified around notions of divinely ordained places and ranked orders; and early industrial culture was unified around work, order and rationalization. However, contemporary culture is, as we have seen, disunified. The TES is ruled by efficiency, rationality, orderliness and discipline while the culture is governed by immediate gratification of the senses and emotions and the indulgence of the undisciplined self.

As Chapter 3 also indicates the pattern of change in culture is a *ricorso*.[2] The human condition or predicament exerts an 'inner pull' that drags people back to a consideration of the meaning of their situation and their existence.[3] Culture is constituted by,

> the wheel of questions that brings one back to the existential predicaments, the awareness in men of their finiteness and the inexorable limits to their power ... and the consequent effort to find a coherent answer to reconcile them to the human condition. [CCC: xxix]

Because the human condition is unchanging these questions of meaning are universal across human cultures. But unlike Parsons' conception of cultural universals (1956) they are not evolutionary. Cultures can elaborate and expand but they will not necessarily do so in a unilinear fashion. They will always need to address the fundamental questions but not always in the same ways. The elements of the human predicament that provide these universal threads of culture are as follows:

- order, the search for regularities in the physical and social universes;
- creation, the search for a point of physical and social origin;
- group identity, the attempt to establish a distinction between oneself and one's own and others;
- courage, a capacity to confront adversity;
- fate and chance;
- instruction, a commitment to teaching the young;
- aesthetics, a capacity for decoration and imagery;
- the sacred, a search for transcendent sources of meaning;
- ritual, engaging in acts that unite the social with the sacred; and
- death, finding meaning in grief and disposal of the corpse.[4]

The institutions of culture can now easily be specified in terms of responding to these needs. They include science, education, ethnicity, philosophy, art and, above all, religion. Religions are the earliest and longest-standing responses, and Bell believes that even the current process of secularization will eventually lose its force because: 'The exhaustion of Modernism, the aridity of Communist life, the tedium of the unrestrained self, and the meaninglessness of monolithic political chants, all indicate that a long era is coming to a slow close' (CCC: xxix).

This explanation for culture now, it seems, verges on the functionalist but Bell wants to plead 'not guilty': 'I do not (*pace* Durkheim) see religion as a "functional necessity" for society, or that without religion a society will dissolve. I do not believe in religion as a patch for the unravelled seams of society' (CCC:

xxviii).[5] This is partly accurate. Bell is, as he says, not a Durkheimian or Radcliffe-Brownian religious functionalist but, as it happens, the explanation does resonate well with Malinowski (e.g. 1939). The need that religion functions to meet is, in Bell, not social but psychological and cultural cohesion. As in Malinowski (1939) the origin of religion lies in anxiety at the level of personality about predicaments provided by the environment – they grow 'out of the deepest needs of individuals' (CCC: xxix) – although, to be sure, in Malinowski the predicaments are much more material than in Bell. More importantly, Bell's belief that without religion culture dissolves can be confirmed by an examination of his argument that secular modernism and postmodernism succeeds in the diremption of culture (see subsequent sections of this chapter for details).

BOURGEOIS CULTURE

The reference point for Bell's critique of contemporary culture is the bourgeois morality that arose in early capitalist society and that was underpinned by Protestantism (CCC: 54–61). The latter encompassed two phenomena: a Protestant ethic, a commitment to work as an end in itself; and a puritan temper, a commitment to an orderly and ascetic lifestyle. They emphasized then, 'work, sobriety, frugality, sexual restraint, and a forbidding attitude towards life' (CCC: 55). In their American manifestation they were associated with the institutions established by the New England pilgrims: farms, mercantilism, artisanship, the nuclear family and, above all, the small town. The growth of the boisterous immigrant cities and the feudalism of the *ante-bellum* South notwithstanding, Bell insists that: 'The life and character of American society were shaped by the small town, and its religions' (CCC: 56). Small towns were highly effective institutions in shaping value-commitments because they could enforce codes of behaviour by means of community sanctions. Puritanical religions could also restrain material demands in the context of a subsistence economy.

Bell sums up the core values of American culture, the Protestant Ethic and the puritan temper, in the thought and actions of two exemplary figures, the theologian Jonathan Edwards and the much-lionized Benjamin Franklin. The Calvinist flight to America had been a rejection of the evils of civilization and its temptations. The relationship to God was direct and unmediated by such human institutions as the corrupt church. But a hundred years of colonization had weakened Calvinist commitments, especially to the personal covenant with God that demanded from each person a life in imitation of Christ. Edwards insisted on the traditional Calvinist precepts, that the shared descent from Adam renders everyone open to depravity and that only the few, the elect, can rise above this. However, this election is demonstrable not by a Weberian accomplishment in the world of work but by the conversion effects of the gift of grace – not by their works but by their faith shall ye know them.

Franklin, by contrast, was engaged in the world of work, constantly calculating and encouraging himself and others to ensure that neither time nor talent nor energy were wasted but that all would be employed usefully. He established an explicit moral calculus based on thirteen useful virtues: temperance, silence, order, resolution, frugality, industry, sincerity, justice, moderation, cleanliness, tranquillity, chastity and humility. Bell affirms that: 'There is perhaps no better inventory of the American creed' (CCC: 58). However, he is not entirely seduced by Franklin, reminding us that Franklin's business success came not merely from thrift and industry but from a cunning capacity to cultivate influence that would be the envy of Norman Vincent Peale, and from a capacity for self-advertisement. And Edwards would not have been impressed by Franklin's habit of parenting illegitimate children, much less by some of the practices involved. There are thus contradictory elements in bourgeois morality: Franklin's positive commitment to profitable expediency and Edwards' obsessive negation of moral depravity.

This opposition did not appear to confound the communities that were established on the basis of the theology. In another functionalist formulation that is, indeed, rather reminiscent of Durkheim, Bell finds that the rational morality of the community was imposed by 'a cold and righteous necessity' (CCC: 59). The Protestants had founded closed communities in an unforgiving environment and this posed both psychological strains and material dangers. All individuals, Bell argues, had to commit themselves to community norms because to sin imperilled not only individual salvation but group cohesion. The social control system that enforced this hard set of rules involved public confession and repentance through self-scourging. This was entirely necessary, argues Bell, because of a 'bucolic realism' about sex and because sins of the flesh would always become visible in a small-scale community. The Puritans therefore became great repenters.

Although the theology was more or less confined to New England, the morality was not. As the society expanded westwards, new settlements faced similar functional problems: 'The towns that were established, first in the wilderness and then in the prairies, faced the problem of maintaining some social order among a population that often had a high proportion of social misfits and ne'er-do-wells' (CCC: 60). Bell makes the rather doubtful claim that town elites that were too small to control deviants by incarceration or exile would nevertheless be able to do so by the informal means of gossip, shaming and public repentance.[6] Here, puritanism was transformed into a more secular but equally wowserish ideology of respectability but in which moral values continued to be associated with material success. Bell is clear though that it was indeed an ideology in the functional Marxist sense, that is, its rhetoric and symbols supported the power of the dominant class:

> As an idea system, Puritanism underwent a transfiguration over a period of 200 years from rigorous Calvinist predestination, through Edwards' aesthetic illuminations, into the transcendentalism of Emerson, and it finally dissolved into the 'genteel tradition' after the Civil War. [CCC: 61]

It could now legitimize both repressive morality in the small towns and an individualistic capitalist culture elsewhere.

The intellectual justification for puritanism dissipated at around the turn of the century under a withering attack from a group at Harvard College, the 'Young Intellectuals', who demanded a more open, inclusive and pleasurable cultural scene. But, in a discussion that is important in Bell's explanation for right-wing political extremism (see Chapter 4), he argues that in the small towns it survived and was even reinforced – the big cities were increasingly 'sinful', the urban intellectuals 'morally feckless'. The backlash took the form of the Temperance movement that became a symbol for the cultural struggle between rural WASP society and an industrializing America based on immigration. For Bell, the critical feature that differentiates the Temperance movement from earlier forms of puritanism is its insistence on the coercion of Prohibition, rather than informal sanctions, as the means of social control. Bell is deeply critical of the development: 'The affirmation and confidence of nineteenth-century life had soured into a constricted and crabbed fear of the future' (CCC: 64). However, Temperance could not succeed against the great social structural changes that were now in train – the demographic predominance of the industrial cities and the emergence of a consumption culture simply made it unworkable.

Bell can now perform the opening stanzas of his cultural-contradictions argument (CCC: 65). In the early-eighteenth-century culture and social structure had been fused – Protestant values matched a pioneering social structure. But the culture was progressively weakened in the face of an emerging liberal middle class. In the prohibition movement, the old status-group sought to use political means to reassert its predominance but it no longer had a socio-economic base from which to mount its challenge. With the defeat of prohibition puritan values lost much of their legitimacy.[7]

MODERNITY

We can now locate this interpretation of early American culture within Bell's general analysis of modernity. He defines it thus: 'Modernity is individualism, the effort of individuals to remake themselves, and, where necessary, to remake society in order to allow design and choice' (1990a: 72). It implies the rejection of any 'naturally' ascribed or divinely ordained order, of external authority, and of collective authority in favour of the self as the sole point of reference for action. Although not every sociologist would agree with him, Bell adduces that sociology frames five important propositions about modernity (1990a: 43–4):

- that society is constructed out of a social contract between individuals;
- that human beings are dualistic, having an original self and an imposed social self, and therefore face the prospect of self-estrangement or alienation;
- that religion is a superstition that precludes self-awareness;
- that modernity involves an autonomization of the value-spheres of culture (art, morality and justice) that, in particular, involves the differentiation of economics from morality and art from religion; and
- that human nature is not universal but that the character of

any particular human being is determined by their location in the social structure (by occupation, ethnicity, gender, etc.).

Under modernity there can be no question about the moral authority of the self. The only question is that of how the self is to be fulfilled – by hedonism, by acquisitiveness, by faith, by the privatization of morality or by sensationalism.

If the Protestant ethic and the puritan temper were the privatized-moralistic answer to this question, the shift to a more hedonistic response, Bell argues, could only be confirmed once modernizing changes had also taken place in the realm of social (techno-economic) structure. The transformation of modern culture is due, he now asserts, 'singularly' to the emergence of mass consumption and the increased affluence of lower socio-economic groups (CCC: 66). The techno-economic changes that made mass consumption possible and desirable began in the 1920s. They were of two types: technological and sociological. A key technological development was the multiplication of human effort by the application of electrical power to manufacturing and to domestic tasks. Others took place in the areas of transportation and the mass media, the latter in the forms of the cinema and radio. The sociological inventions were, for Bell, even more profound. They were: the moving assembly line that reduced the cost of consumer durables, especially cars; the development of advertising and marketing systems that could cultivate consumer taste; and the extension of consumer credit through instalment plans, hire purchase, personal loans, and the like. These spelt the end of Protestant bourgeois culture.

One of the structural characteristics that had preserved small-town morality was that, notwithstanding the railroads that were their lifelines, they were highly isolated. The availability of cheap personal transportation ended this isolation forever. People, especially young people, could begin to escape moral oversight either temporarily or permanently. The automobile also offered other interesting possibilities: 'The closed car became the *cabinet particulier* of the middle class, the place where adventurous young people could shed their sexual inhibitions and broke the old taboos' (CCC: 67). But the sophisticated and sinful world of modernity was also penetrating these communities directly by means of the growing mass media. The movies brought a fantasy world that stressed gratification of the emotions through romance and consumption. Radio brought these options directly into Protestant domesticity and, more importantly, seduced the God-fearing into the evils of materialism by means of advertising.

Bell is certain that advertising played a crucial role in the cultural transformation of America. It not only cultivated new wants and demands but also, in a process of resocialization, created an entirely new lifestyle: 'Against frugality, selling emphasized prodigality; against asceticism, the lavish display' (CCC: 69). The earliest consequences were new tastes and manners, but eventually advertising reconstituted women and the young as independent consumers, undermined traditional and familistic bases of authority, and redefined achievement in terms of capacity to consume rather than capacity to produce. A critical development that made this lifestyle possible was the availability of easy credit that depended only on the capacity to repay provided by a steady income rather than on collateral assets. Nothing did more to undermine the moral habits of Protestantism that focused on abstinence and saving. Debt went from being a source of shame to becoming a central component of lifestyle.

The result was the emergence of a distinctive civilization that Bell gives us the option of calling either a 'mass society' or an 'industrial society' and that defines what he calls a revolution in sensibility (CCC: 88–91). This new sensibility is governed by four societal characteristics:

- *Number.* The USA has a large population that is relatively interconnected. People know and know of far more other people than they did in the past.
- *Interaction.* The interconnections between people, through travel, larger work units, housing density and mass mediation, have multiplied so that society is more 'dense'.
- *Self-consciousness.* Identity no longer comes from family origins but from personal experience, reflection and orientation: 'A person today says, "I am I, I come out of myself, and in choice and action I make myself".'[8] This experience tends to the generational rather than the familial.
- *Time-orientation.* Society is no longer crescive but future-orientated, with an emphasis on biographical as well as societal planning.

The first two of these lead to an emphasis in cultural sensibility on immediacy, impact, sensation and simultanity, while the last two have become modes of experience in themselves.

Bell's conservative orientation to the culture of mass society can now emerge. In describing the hedonistic cultural syndrome he deploys such words as 'fantasy' and 'make-believe'. In arguments that are reminiscent of the Frankfurt School[9] he thereby constructs the consumer as a dupe who lives in a fantasy world in the future. Although he would deny the parallel, Bell's contemporary consumer bears a pronounced similarity to Weber's salvation-hungry Protestant, chained to the treadmill of work and fruitlessly pursuing the fantasies of paradise if, on this occasion, an earthly paradise. But for Bell, the consumer rather than the worker is compulsive and self-delusional, because of a resolute focus on play, fun and pleasure. Bell reserves special attention for the way in which sex has become the main vehicle for these possibilities: *Playboy* is successful because it offers men fantasies of sexual prowess; California is the epitomistic 'State of excitement'; and vacations are advertised as opportunities for unusual sexual encounters. With a tinge of prudish nostalgia, he therefore proposes that, 'the cult of the Orgasm succeeded the cult of Mammon as the basic passion of American life' (CCC: 70).

In more formal terms, Bell's critique of modernity centres on the absence of a moral or transcendental ethic that is displaced by a mere individualized anxiety. In puritan communities guilt was assuaged by repentance. In mass society anxiety is assuaged by psychotherapy, a process that for Bell is bound to fail because security of identity can only be accomplished within a moral context. This transformation is but one consequence of the contradictions that arise from the cultural developments of modernity. The primary contradiction, as Chapter 2 indicates, lies between cultural norms of hedonism and social structural norms of work discipline. But there is also an enormous contradiction within the social structure itself: a good worker delays gratification but a good consumer looks for immediate gratification. Bell concludes that this means: 'One is to be "straight" by day and a "swinger" by night'; and then cannot resist an exclamatory protest: 'This is self-fulfilment and self-realization!' (CCC: 72).

MODERNISM[10]

This brings Bell to, 'an extraordinary sociological puzzle', that of why the cultural movement of modernism that repeatedly attacks and dirempts modern social structure and bourgeois culture should have persisted in the face of this contradiction for more than a century. He defines modernism as: 'the self-willed effort of a style and sensibility to remain in the forefront of "advancing consciousness" ' (CCC: 46). This attempt can be expressed in terms of several possible descriptions. First it can be described as avant garde, as rejecting elitist cultural traditions in favour of a re-insertion of life into art. Second, it is adversarial: 'The legend of modernism is that of the free creative spirit at war with the bourgeoisie' (CCC: 40). This often places its practitioners in a peculiar relationship with the *status quo* in which they both attack it and depend upon it. Last, it is impenetrable within contemporary understandings and requires intellectual gyrations to be appreciated: 'It is wilfully opaque, works with unfamiliar forms, is self-consciously experimental, and seeks deliberately to disturb the audience – to shock it, shake it up, even to transform it as if in a religious conversion' (CCC: 46). This gives modernism an esoteric appeal, as Bell intones slightly ironically, but it also denies its other claims to being adversarial and avant garde – an elitist indulgence can be nothing but privileged.

The tone of modernism was set by groups of avant-garde artists doing innovative and experimental work with which they would taunt a complacent bourgeois audience. The tension between artist and audience was therefore central to the work of such groups as those French Impressionists who first exhibited in their *Salon des refusés*. However, by the mid-twentieth century American abstract expressionism was rejecting its audience entirely and becoming, 'preoccupied with problems of structure and medium – breaking away from the easel, using paint itself as a subject for art, involving the artist's own person in the painting – of a special and esoteric nature outside the experience of the layman' (CCC: 39). In modernism content and form disappear in favour of medium as the central expression. In art the stress is on paint, its means of application and possible substitutes for it; music stresses sounds rather than harmony; poetry emphasises 'breath' and phonemics; literature employs wordplay as against plot or genre; drama promotes action and spectacle at the expense of characterization.

As is discussed above, modernism was a rage against a bourgeois order. That 'legend', as Bell calls it, has now been extended to order of all kinds. The free, creative spirit of the artist is now at war with, ' "civilization" or "repressive tolerance" or some other agency that curtails "freedom" ' (CCC: 40). This adversarial strategy has, in general, been highly successful. The modern cultural arena has divorced from the capitalist system that spawned it and has become self-referential. The 'hierophants of culture' now construct the audience and in dominating and exploiting it have come to constitute a cultural class. They can be called a class, Bell argues, for three reasons (CCC: 41): they have grown sufficiently in number to establish group networks and not to be treated as deviant; they have completely defeated the opposition – there is no longer any bourgeois high culture to attack; and they have independent control of the material substructure of artistic expression – galleries, film studios, weekly magazines, universities, and so on. From this lofty salient they sally forth to mount their attacks on crusty tradition:

> Today, each new generation, starting off at the benchmarks attained by the adversary culture of its cultural parents, declares in sweeping fashion that the status quo represents backward conservatism or repression, so that in a widening gyre, new and fresh assaults on the social structure are mounted. [CCC: 41]

The emphasis on medium and the rage against order are two of the three dimensions of contemporary modernism that Bell isolates. However, the third dimension, what he calls 'the eclipse of distance' (CCC: 108–119), is the one to which he gives the most attention. The classical fine arts followed two central principles: they were rational in that they organized space and time into a consistent and unified expression; and they were mimetic in that they sought to mirror or represent life and nature. Modernism denies these externalities and emphasizes instead the interior life, rejecting the constraints of the world and glorifying expressions of the self. Bell repeats the terms sensation, simultaneity, immediacy and impact, as the syntax of modernism. Against the contemplative character of classical art, each of the artistic modernist movements (Impressionism, Post-Impressionism, Futurism, Expressionism and Cubism) intends:

> on the syntactical level, to break up ordered space; in its aesthetic, to bridge the distance between object and spectator, to 'thrust' itself on the viewer and establish itself immediately by impact. One does not interpret the scene; instead, one feels it as a sensation and is caught up by that emotion. [CCC: 112]

Bell finds similar syntactical and aesthetic patterns in literature and music. Modern literature seeks to plunge the reader into the maelstrom of the emotions while music abandons structure in its entirety.

Bell can now formalize his idea that the eclipse of distance is central to modernism. The process takes three expressions. First, there is a loss of psychic distance. Following Freud, Bell argues that a mature personality is able to make a distinction between the past (and its horrors) and the present, and to recognize that the past is over and gone. Modernist culture disrupts this differentiation and thereby prevents a sense of climax or overcoming. Second, there is a loss of aesthetic distance in which the artist seeks to place the audience at the centre of the art, to have them experience art rather than engage in dialogue with it. For Bell, film is a critical modern medium because its huge screens and darkened viewing area can accomplish just this effect. Third, there is a loss of social distance, in so far as the artist and the audience are engaged in a common experience. All this amounts to an attempt to dramatize the moment by offering psychedelic experiences that place one at the edge of madness. Bell is unimpressed, because the mundane routineness of everyday life remains vacant of a meaning that modernism cannot offer.

> In the theater the curtain falls, the play ends. In life one has to go home, go to bed, awaken the next morning, brush one's teeth, wash one's face, shave, defecate, and go to work. Everyday time is different from psychedelic time; and how far can the disjunction be stretched? [CCC: 118]

We can now connect modernism with the three-realms argument. The disjunctions between culture and social structure are sustained by a mutual divorce. The cognitive expressions that arise from the social (techno-economic) structure are rapidly reifying and rationalizing human experience: extreme levels of occupational differentiation separate persons from the roles that they occupy; the proliferation of knowledge subcultures prevents the formation of single expressive tradition that can speak to all; and the mathematization of symbolic representations leaves society without a common cultural language. Modernism is itself complicit in this development because, in rejecting the possibility of a common style, it prevents any claim that it is a culture at all. Modernist culture is differentiating rapidly into a variety of 'demesnes'; it lacks authoritative centres, it focuses on the instant-aneity of the visual, electronic media rather than the permanence of print, and it denies the rationality of the cosmos. The out-come of these dual forces is the diremption of culture as an idea. In an important sense, Bell regards modern society as a society without a culture.

POSTMODERNISM

If Bell is worried about the effects of modernism then he is positively horrified by the prospects implied by the rise of post-modernism. Bell regards postmodernism as an essentially mod-ernist trend but as one which carries modernist logic to extremes. Postmodernism substitutes instinctual and erotic justifications for aesthetic and humanistic ones. In the hands of Foucault and Brown:[11] 'It announced not only the "de-construction of Man" and the end of the humanist credo, but also the "epistemological break" with genitality and the dissolution of focused sexuality into the polymorph perversity of oral and anal pleasures' (1990a: 69). It legitimated both homosexual liberation and a hippie-rock-drug culture, the latter striking directly at the motivational system that sustains an industrial or post-industrial TES. In a jaundiced phrase, Bell notes that, 'the culturati, ever ready, follow[ed] the winds of fashion' (1990a: 70) as artists and architects took up the slogan to attack the boundary between high and popular culture. Postmodernist art, architecture and music emphasize pas-tiche and playfulness, in Bell's view, at the expense of creativity and genuine style.

Postmodernism was the product that arose out of the particu-lar 'sensibility' of the decade of the 1960s. Within this sensibility, the modernist stress on the self was repeated in a more strident and harsher tone. But the 1960s added ingredients of their own: an interest in violence as entertainment; a flight from 'normal' heterosexuality; loud music; anti-intellectualism; and a determi-nation to erase the boundaries between art, life, and politics (CCC: 121–3). The outcome was dire in cultural terms. Bell sets out the consequences under four persuasive epigrammatical headings:

- *The dissolution of 'art'.* Traditional art, as we have seen, involves objectification by the artist and distanciation between the audience and the object. In the 1960s artists redefined art as action, that is, as an event or happening or performance, rather than as an object. This was especially true in sculpture, that now involved not the creation of objects but the rearrangement of spaces, forms, media, time and light into such happenings. Equally, painting became 'environmental', moving out from the restrictions of the flat canvas, initially by collage but eventually into human habitats.

- *The democratization of genius*. Traditional culture involves hierarchies of taste in the top echelons of which heroic figures, artistic geniuses, can set new standards of judgement. Because postmodernism celebrates emotion rather than intellect it, first, implies that all cultural products are of equal value, and, second, that the authenticity of such products must be established according to the immediacy of their expression and impact. Thus: 'The democratization of genius is made possible by the fact that while one can quarrel with judgements one cannot quarrel with feelings' (CCC: 134). No expressed set of feelings can be held to be authoritative but equally none is without value.

- *The loss of self*. Traditional literature, especially the novel, focuses on the self and the centrality of its experience as an indicator of the human condition. In the 1960s the self disappeared from literature in favour of a preoccupation with what Bell can only describe as 'madness'. Novels became hallucinatory, schizoid, nihilistic, depressive, apocalyptic and feculent. The self was colonized by impersonal forces, by corporeal transformations and by chemicals.

- *The Dionysiac pack*. Here Bell speaks to the transformation of theatre. Drama is traditionally confined to a determinate space and a cast and dialogue that are specified by a text. The new theatre of the 1960s distrusted text entirely so that players, in effect, became playwrights. It aimed for spontaneity and shock, and frequently sought physically to mix actors and audiences. And, in its most extreme form, it sought immediacy and impact by the literal enactment of violence on stage. Bell is disgusted because: 'Traditionally, violence has been repugnant to the intellectual as a confession of failure' (CCC: 142).

By the 1970s the counterculture of the 1960s had all but dissolved. Painting once again became representational and sculpture became technological, but drama and literature became aimless. The reason, Bell argues, is not for want of rebellion but for want of some restraint against which to rebel. Rebellion became orthodox. Bell is convinced that modernism reached its apogee in the 1920s and that the 1960s were just its last aspiration. Postmodernism, the cultural legacy of the 1960s, is the mere shell of a culture:

> What passes for serious culture today lacks both content and form, so that the visual arts are primarily decorative and literature a self-indulgent babble or contrived experiment. Decoration, by its nature, no matter how bright and gay, becomes, in its finite and repetitive patterns, mere wallpaper, a receding background incapable of engaging the viewer in the renewable re-visions of perception. Self-referential literature, when both the self and the referent repeat the same old refrains, becomes a tedious bore, like Uno in the circus, showing that he can raise himself on one finger. A culture of re-cycled images and twice-told tales is a culture that has lost its bearings. [1990a: 70]

RELIGION

At one level CCC is a thesis for the restoration of religion – as Bell says, for him religion is the 'fulcrum' of the book (CCC: xxviii). The working-out of modernism results in the diremption of culture in the important specific sense that it denies the possibility of religion. However, its spiralling decline, its deflated vacuity presents an opportunity for revival: 'I believe that a culture which has become aware of its limits in exploring the mundane will turn, at some point, to the effort to recover the sacred' (CCC: xxix). We can here explore Bell's argument about the transformation of religion and the return of the sacred (1971b; CCC: 146–61; WP: 324–54).

As we have seen, all cultural formations are answers to the fundamental questions of human existence. However, religion differs from other formations in that it organizes its answers coherently and explicitly into a creed, provides rituals that bind together the members with emotional ties and sets up an organized institution that can expansively reproduce the creed and its rituals (WP: 333–4). Although he would distance himself from functional*ism*, Bell indicates that, historically, religion has had two functions in Western society: first, it 'guarded the portals of the demonic', that is, it specified and excluded the evil and destructive; and second, it provided a moral connection with the past by means of tradition (CCC: 157). For this reason, the great religions that overarch Western culture have always stressed legal and moral restraint on profligacy, sexuality and violence.

Since the emergence of capitalism religion has undergone two great transformations. The first of these is the sociologically familiar one of secularization. Bell's version is similar to that offered in structural-functional accounts, that is, he views secularization not as a decline in religious practice or belief but rather as a shrinking of the institutional authority of religion from the public sphere of art and politics to the private sphere of church and family. Indeed, even though secularization is supported by rationalization in the TES, it implies no necessary lack of vigour or commitment in religious action in these private spheres. In modern secularized societies religious revivalism is endemic.

Bell's second transformation, the one that attracts more of his interest, is akin to Weber's notion of disenchantment. Between the seventeenth and nineteenth centuries Western societies went through a 'Great Profanation', 'the attenuation of a theodicy as providing a set of meanings to explain man's relation to the beyond' (CCC: 167). The Great Profanation is associated with the rise of a modernism that commits itself to transgression and to the violation of taboos until there is, well, 'nothing sacred'. It embraces three components (WP: 334–7):

- Radical individualism in the TES and the polity and an unrestrained self in the culture.
- A shift from religion to fine arts as the arena within which moral questions are answered so that demonic impulses have become 'polymorph perverse' – all sins have become the stuff of fantasy, violence has become the aesthetic of politics, and passion mere carnal sensuality.
- A rise in nihilism, the belief that there is nothing 'beyond', no ultimate source of meaning, no transcendence, so that human beings are caught between the imminent and the void – but mortality remains the ultimate test of meaning and the modern inability to comprehend the annihilation of that self that it worships smothers the creative consciousness.

The Great Profanation opened a space for the development of alternatives to religion. Bell lists five: rationalism, aestheticism, existentialism, civil religions and political religions (WP: 338). He addresses two of these, aestheticism and political religions, in detail and finds that they both fail. Aestheticism (of which Baudelaire is Bell's main exemplar) fails because it can offer neither externality nor guidance, since to be guided by the will or the passion can only leave one without a sense of direction. Such political religions as communism (of which here Bell addresses Lukács as the exemplar) fail because they cannot provide a set of ultimate values that will prevent human beings from following their demonic impulses. Communist regimes inevitably corrupt in the direction of authoritarianism and state terrorism. The humanitarian Lukács himself even succumbed.

For Bell, the Great Profanation will inevitably be succeeded by the 'Great Instauration', the restoration of religion as a central principle of culture because 'the existential questions of culture are inescapable' (WP: 353). Distancing himself from Weber, he reckons that the return of religion will not take the puritanizing path of earlier religious transformations. Rather, the new religion will be a genuine revival, a return to a tradition that will connect the individual with the past and the future. In the West, he argues, it will take three forms (WP: 349–50):

- *Moralizing religion.* This will be a return to a fundamentalist faith that exposes the morally feckless and acts as a restraint on any possibility of complete personal freedom. It will be a puritan revival that emerges in its traditional rural and lower-middle-class heartlands.

- *Redemptive religion.* This will be a recovery of the moral ground that has been lost, a rediscovery of the past on an intellectual level by the urban middle class. It will recognize that individuals owe debts to the families, communities and institutions that gave them their moral awareness. The institutional structure of such religion, focused on communities, will intercalate between its members and remote and anomic large-scale bureaucracies and governments. This will be a lifeworld religion providing a mutually caring environment.

- *Mythic religion.* This will likely be Oriental in origin. It will provide for the re-enchantment of an overly rationalized and scientistic world. It will employ symbols as focuses for the discovery of unity of form and purpose in apparently contradictory and hostile events and modes of expression. A recommitment to mythical symbols can re-establish that unity of culture

– of the natural world, of human expression and of ultimate meanings – that religion traditionally provides.

From Bell's point of view this is an optimistic note on which to end his analysis of culture, certainly one that is full of personal possibilities.

CONCLUSION

Bell's analysis of culture is a dazzling *tour de force*, a brilliant demonstration of his humanity, his intellect, his passion and his sensitivity. The work is challenging, stimulating, informative and, as one has come to expect from Bell, prescient. Although it has the familiar Bellian problems of repetition, conceptual looseness and inconsistency, these apparent deficiencies seem to provide him with a freedom to range across the regions of culture with a facility that no other sociologist has remotely accomplished. Above all, CCC is riveting and inspiring to read. The reason for this is that Bell is deeply steeped in canonical Western culture and in his own Jewish religion and therefore feels the diremption of culture and the loss of religion in an acutely personal way. The link between passion and intellect is reflected in the writing. This being the case, perhaps this reader-author can respond equally personally. Although, as I have made clear, Bell's interpretation of modern culture is devastatingly brilliant, the argument is both sociologically and normatively problematic.

The conclusion to Chapter 3 of this book indicates the socio-logical problems. Everywhere Bell finds radical contradictions between developments that do not really contradict each other at all. The biggest disjunction apparently lies between a culture that celebrates the self and a TES that requires the subordination of the self to discipline. However, an alternative interpretation of these events is possible. In such an interpretation, the TES does not require discipline in the sense of vocation or asceticism as specified by early Calvinism, it requires discipline in the sense of a non-internalized conformity to rules. It accomplishes this conformity by delivering material gratifications, mediated by wages, to the privatized individual. The individual negotiates a career through the TES by 'economizing' the relative values of wages, promotions, meaningful work, leisure time, overtime, etc. The primary source of commitment in the TES is indeed therefore a radicalized individualism that links firmly to the gratification of the untrammelled self. On this alternative view, the fit between the instrumental worker, the yuppie entrepreneur, the rapacious consumer and a spectacular, de-hierarchized artistic arena is indissoluble.

We can argue the reverse in relation to the Protestant ethic and puritan temper. Bell regards them as the foundation of the American value-system. In fact, they might more usefully be regarded as standing in contradiction to that system. Bell writes as if the immigrant cities, the golden West, and the sunbelt (and, had it not been subordinated, the deep South), are marginal appendages to small towns. But surely the American value-system is precisely located in the Hollywood fantasies of its East European immigrant moguls, in the get-rich-quick entrepreneurialism of its Irish railway builders, in the organized crime and political corruption of its great cities and, indeed, in the Eastern liberal establishment. Small-town America is a temporary aberration that occasionally surfaces as religious fundamentalism or political extremism. It is really this puritanism that is un-American because it insists on the importance of the collectivity and the subordination of the individual. Certainly, it would be difficult to regard Protestant bourgeois culture as a source of tradition because it is a cleansing, reformist movement that itself rejects authoritative hierarchies. Indeed, nowhere else but in America has tradition been driven out quite so thoroughly and universally because there was so little of it to evict. Modernism and postmodernism were entirely consistent with American values and indeed have flourished there on an heroic level unmatched in any other part of the world. This is perhaps the reason that Jameson (1984), far from seeing postmodernism as a contradiction of capitalism, sees it as capitalism's cultural logic.

Bell's explanation for the rise of modernism is that technology released the demonic self from its religious gaol. Several full-blown alternative arguments suggest that the 'self', demonic or otherwise, is a modern construction rather than a foundational reality. Foucault (1981), for example, argues that sexuality was not constrained under premodern conditions but rather was embedded within kinship. For him, bourgeois society 'discovered' sexuality and defined its perversities so that it could control it, precisely by means of discipline. For Foucault, as for Giddens (1985), discipline and surveillance are central components of modern societies, institutionalized in schools, prisons, hospitals, universities and the state as well as factories. Bell tells us that bourgeois culture had long since been defeated by the 1960s so that there was nothing against which to rebel, but Foucault tells us that there remained a society replete with authoritarian practices, elitist imposts and bureaucratic controls. If the self strains to express itself against such constraints it is surely a little dismissive to treat that effort as inauthentic or as mere opinionism. Certainly, it would be difficult to conceive of postmodernist cultural products as inauthentic judged against, say, landscape, still life, operatic kitsch or musical Romanticism.

Bell's value-stance on culture is not merely conservative but elitist. His derogations of popular culture, of the democratization of genius and of postmodernism represent a claim not merely for authoritative but for authoritarian cultural standards. The most liberal reading of Bell's argument would suggest that he is claiming only that cultural standards must be set by knowledgeable experts who have worked through the canon and drawn upon the accumulated wisdom of generations. Three counter-arguments might be offered. First, as a reading of Bourdieu (1984) suggests, expertise is intimately linked to structures of power and class. The operation of systems of expertise acts as a mechanism of closure on access to privilege. For what it is worth, the dedifferentiation of high and popular culture entailed in postmodernism has almost certainly increased the level of openness in occupational hierarchies. Second, while expertise may briefly have been a neutral arbiter of cultural worth it has long since been commodified along with that art on which it pronounces. Expert opinion is now directly translatable into monetary values so that the quality of a cultural object reflects its price and not vice versa. One can no longer find either good cheap art or bad expensive art. Therefore, it might seem an appropriate time not to mourn the demise of standards but to applaud the fact that standards are set in the market place, in as democratic a fashion as that institution will allow. Third, it is arguable that expertise and a fixation on tradition smother innovation and participation. From an egalitarian or liberationist perspective it matters little that postmodernism may have been a failed experiment so long as the artistic market place remains as open as it can possibly be to both producers and consumers. In sum, Bell might be falling victim to the tendency of what Habermas calls the hermeneutic sciences to defend, 'sterilized knowledge against the reflective appropriation of active traditions and [lock] history up in a museum' (1972: 316).

Bell's sociology of religion is susceptible to a similar critique.

One can sympathize with the yearning of a prodigal son to re-establish a connection with the tradition of his parents, but it does not necessarily make for a coherent sociological position. Bell draws parallels between his Great Profanation and Weber's notion of disenchantment, but he failed to appropriate from Weber the irreversibility of disenchantment once in train. One cannot learn faith or create religion by reflexive acts of communitas or philosophical appropriation. The saliency of religion is only effective under conditions of habituation or transcendental experience. As Weber tells us, there will be no Great Instauration, and if that means a long dark night of the soul then that is the price of self-knowledge. However, even if there was a major religious restoration one might want to consider whether it was indeed value-positive. Bell is fully aware of the negatives of puritanism, not to mention political ideology, but why he fails to extend these to all systems of thought that turn human beings into the cringing subordinates of the whims of hypostatized powers, personal or natural, is entirely unclear. For all the economic and political constraints imposed by modernization, what Weber and Habermas tell us is that it at least holds out the possibility of the predominance of human reason over tradition and superstition and thus the prospect of social and political emancipation. In Europe, as Habermas (1992) successfully shows, early *Bürgerliche Gesellschaft* was an expression of freedom to hold and express opinion and to undertake action under a relaxation of religious constraints. Indeed, nothing could be more Jeffersonian. Bell's conservatism in culture appears to be calling for a rejection of the possibilities implied by that liberality.

8

Revelations of a Technologized Future

Because he is a central and controversial figure, Bell is often called upon to give interviews by journalists or academics. An obligatory question is the one about what he is working on now, what is going to follow his three big ideas. His usual reply is that he has several new ones, some of which are in bits and pieces 'in the basement' and some of which will be expansions of successful journal articles. A perennial among these is what one interviewer (Chernow 1979: 17) describes as, 'a quasi-futuristic excursion into new computer technology and telecommunications technology and their implications for society'.[1] Bell certainly has enough material to put such a book together and indeed, at the time of writing, a small volume is being planned with Harvard University Press. This chapter seeks to reconstruct what such a book might say.

Prediction and forecasting was the main issue that thrust Bell into public prominence. The 1960s was an era of generational change in which educated and intellectualized baby-boomers were beginning to demand a positive construction of their future lives. The horizon of the future had moved on from the bleak prospect of 1984 to the almost magical possibilities of a new millennium.

The year 2000 was no longer the stuff of science fiction but the tangible vista of a new beginning. In 1964 Bell was appointed by the Kennedy-Johnson administration to be a member of the President's Commission on Technology, Automation and Economic Progress. In the same year he was instrumental in persuading the American Academy of Arts and Sciences to set up a *Commission on the Year 2000*. Bell became the chairman of this ten-year project on forecasting the future to which some fifty of the leading social scientists and other intellectuals in the USA contributed. In 1979 he was appointed by President Carter as a member of the Commission on a National Agenda for the 1980's.[2]

Bell has recently returned to prediction and forecasting, especially in relation to technology, in his retirement. He writes journalistic essays that are published first in Japanese or Korean and then re-issued in English in the Journal *Dissent*. Because they are both accessible and insightful they are often included in collections put together for first-year students. All this suggests that Bell remains an authority on the shape of the future, despite the fact that he has very real doubts about whether one can say anything accurate about it all. We can begin then by examining Bell's views on what forms of prediction and forecasting are possible in the social sciences.

PREDICTION AND FORECASTING

For Bell, prediction is both an inevitable consequence of the coming of post-industrial society and a moral imperative. The post-industrial society is a planning society that has at its disposal an intellectual technology that can assimilate vast amounts of data, analyse them as 'what ... if ... then' scenarios, and isolate trends and make projections. Bell's liberalism prescribes the moral imperative in that planning can expand choice. Here he distances himself once again from a Marxist historicism that would view the future as determined and inevitable. Rather, that future is an open field: 'One seeks "pre-vision" as much to "halt" a future as help it come into being, for the function of prediction is not, as often stated, to aid social control, but to widen the spheres of moral choice' (1964: 873).

Unfortunately, the whole field is rather hazardous because the future is, in large measure, unknowable. This is particularly true of what Bell (1965b) calls 'point events', specific occurrences that singly can alter the pattern of historical change, especially where they are the consequence of decisions taken by the individual incumbents of powerful positions. Save some hopeful emigrés, few predicted the radical reconstruction of Eastern Europe and the Soviet Union in the late 1980s because there was nothing inevitable about the specific conjunction of decisions made by Gorbachev and Yeltsin. Even in the unlikely circumstance of perfect knowledge of the intentions of politicians, any political juncture is so full of alternative contingencies that prediction of them is quite impossible. But it is also true of the forecasting of general trends and trajectories based on probability models (COPIS: 4). The further one seeks to project the future, the less accurate one is likely to be, because the uncertain elements in probability models will tend to build on each other and 'fan out' the possible outcomes. Moreover, the models are dependent on point events because human decisions can radically alter the course of history. Forecasts can only be made on the basis of assumptions about the rationality of human decisions, and such assumptions may not reflect actual patterns of prejudice, aggression or interest in the protection of privilege. This means that forecasting can have only the function of establishing the limits within which policy decisions can be made.

Bell surveys four common modes of forecasting (COPIS: 4–6). Technological forecasting can establish rates of change within closed classes of events, say, transportation speeds or the capacity of RAM chips. Of course, it cannot forecast specific inventions or dramatic breakthroughs. By contrast, demographic forecasting has become relatively accurate precisely because the future shape of a population can be witnessed in its current structure of age and gender. Even here the predictions must be made within certain assumptions and parameters, e.g. about the absence or presence of war or stability and change in marriage norms and sexual mores. A third example, economic forecasting, takes three forms: market research that can anticipate demand; the projection of secular trends in macro-economic variables; and econometric models. The latter is an attempt to 'shut out' the intervening effects of social and cultural variables by assuming a closed and rational system. Consequently, it is the victim of a paradox – the more it rejects complexity the more precise it becomes but also the less accurate it becomes. The last example, political forecasting, is, however, in Bell's view, even less accurate.

This is because political developments depend on the motives of politicians and their supporters.

Social forecasting is more important than any of these because the social arena can be thought of as a set of independent variables that 'causes' change in the other arenas. In COPIS (7–9) Bell reduces an earlier list of twelve modes of sociological prediction (1964) to three modes of forecasting. The first mode is trend extrapolation. This, Bell suggests, has limited use in forecasting the future as a whole because trend lines can shift up and down and we cannot determine which particular part of a time-series to project. Equally, extrapolation cannot take account of complex interactions between the time-series variables. The second mode of forecasting is the classical sociological strategy of identifying singular historical keys or laws that will inevitably transform society – the class struggle or bureaucratization or structural differentiation, for example. All of these have failed because each fails to take account of alternative theories. Bell, possibly mistakenly, hold the Weberian drive towards bureaucratization to be inconsistent with a Tocquevillean drive towards equality, for example.

Bell finally arrives at the mode of social forecasting that he favours, theorizing social *frameworks*. These are, 'the structures of the major institutions that order the lives of individuals in a society: the distribution of persons by occupation, the education of the young, the regulation of political conflict, and the like' (COPIS: 8–9). A social framework is a conceptual scheme, rather than a picture of reality, that identifies big transformations – examples include shifts from an agrarian to an industrialized economy or from state socialism to market democracy. Social frameworks have the virtue for forecasting that they are easy to identify and, because the shifts have such inertia, that they are seldom reversed. However, he warns, they do not allow us to predict particular future events but only to specify the agenda of questions that must be solved in the future. Notwithstanding this caveat, and given that the subtitle of COPIS is 'A venture in social forecasting', it will come as no surprise to discover that, for Bell, the key framework for forecasting the future in the contemporary context is 'the post-industrial society' (for discussion see Chapter 6): 'The idea of the post-industrial society . . . is a social forecast about a change in the social framework of Western society' (COPIS: 9). In an unpublished set of notes Bell insists that such a forecast cannot be written as an integrated future scenario or a global model because this would be an exercise in futility, that forecasting is a means of answering specific kinds of theoretical or political questions. Forecasting therefore proceeds in the following way:

> [O]ne should try to define 'axial principles' and 'axial structures' which provide the skeletal structures or the lines of division in a setting. To look for social frameworks and structural contexts that are based on these axial principles. And to 'test for' undertows by seeing what underlying forces may be latent and which can be eruptive under certain conditions. [1978: 1]

Even so, a social framework is only one element in a general social forecast, as an inspection of Bell's attempt to construct one can show (TY2000: 3–7). Here Bell suggests that there are four main sources of change in American society:

- *technology*: here Bell heralds some particular technological developments – biomedical engineering, a national computer network,[3] and climatic modification – but also rehearses COPIS arguments about a new intellectual technology;
- *a wider diffusion of goods and privileges* (including access to higher education);
- *developments in societal structure*: the centralization and nationalization of politics and the post-industrial society; and
- *the relationship of the United States to the rest of the world*.[4]

Taken together these create a set of very real policy issues that read rather like an inventory of the corpus of his work: the problems posed by a more communal society for individual liberty; the strain of bureaucratic controls; the reorganization of business to incorporate the knowledge elite; the decline of the family and threats to privacy; communications overload; and of course, the perennial favourite, the disjunctions between culture and social structure.[5]

THE THIRD TECHNOLOGICAL REVOLUTION

Bell orders the development of technology through time in relation to his post-industrial-society prism, specifying three technological eras that correspond with pre-industrial, industrial and post-industrial society respectively. They are (1992: 15–16):

- *mechanical technology* or applications of natural power sources (animate and environmental) to direct tools including the wheel, the plough, pumps, levers and mills;
- *steam and electric technology* where machines and tools 'embody' the technology without guidance by human muscle power; and
- *intellectual technology* where information is encoded into machines.

The shifts between these types of technology can be described as revolutionary. In the era of mechanical technology tools were worked by co-ordination between the hand and the eye and, while inventors could imagine complex transportation or entertainment devices (such as Leonardo's helicopter), they could not begin to imagine a way to power them. This changed with the 'industrial revolution' that applied power mainly derived from the combustion of fossil fuels to manufacturing. The central devices, the steam engine, the electrical generator and the internal combustion engine, converted carbon into energy that could complement and multiply human effort.

By contrast, the central inventions of intellectual technology are not machines, notwithstanding new devices in computing and telecommunications. The intellectual technology lies behind the machines and is contained in the rules and programmes that control them and the networks of information that link them together. Bell also stresses that the current shift is not merely the overlay of new technology on top of the old industrial technology but rather a complete penetration and reorganization of all fields of economic production. This shift is both organizational, in that downscaling and flexibility tend to debureaucratize firms, and geographical, in that production units become more dispersed.

Bell's sociological argument about technology is not fully worked out. For this reason there is some inconsistency between his various descriptions of technological shifts as revolutions. The movements into each of three eras specified above are described as a revolutionary shift but in TTR (8–12; 1987: 10–12) technological revolutions take on a somewhat different configuration. Here the first revolution is the discovery of steam power that provided a quantum leap in the application of energy to human tasks. The decisive change induced by steam power was that it enabled the development of new methods of production that could multiply productivity and enrich the society. Clearly this coincides with the change from pre-industrial to industrial social structure. However, Bell's second technological revolution takes place at about the turn of the twentieth century and is associated with innovations in chemistry and electricity. Electricity allows the distribution of power over long distances, it provides light and the possibility of rapid communication, while chemistry allows the creation of synthetic dyes, plastics and fabrics. If Bell sticks to the first, three-eras scheme then the electro-chemical innovations cannot qualify as a revolution but if he confirms the TTR scheme, the three-eras scheme needs to be expanded to four by a subdivision of the industrial era.

However, there is absolute consistency about the third technological revolution. It encompasses four technological innovations (TTR: 10–12):

- the replacement of mechanical parts by electronic parts with consequent cost savings, improvements in reliability and exponential reductions in processing time;
- miniaturization, especially in electrical conduction and switching systems;
- digitalization, that is, the conversion of information to binary codes; and
- software, an increasing tendency to use flexible, adaptable instructions that can customize machinery to a wide variety of uses.

However, these technological developments are themselves contingent on a longer-term process that Bell calls the codification of theoretical knowledge (1992: 25–31). By this he means the establishment of theoretical connections between statements of known fact and the organization of these facts into closed symbolic systems. In the industrial era inventions were propelled by the need to produce solutions to immediate practical problems and were therefore made largely in isolation from one another. But in the current, post-industrial era the codification of scientific theory can allow any technological innovation to draw upon and make connections with many others. Bell makes much of the fact that atomic technology, photo-optics, and the accuracy of fine-scale measuring instruments each rely on one of three theoretical papers written by Einstein. Equally, solid-state electronics, radar, semiconductors, and biotechnology rely on the codifications of pure science. Indeed, nowhere has this codification been more effective than in the area of information theory itself that has concentrated on the principles by which one can transform ideas into elements that can be transmitted and manipulated by electronic means.

The technological outcome of these theoretical developments is a technological merger between telecommunications and computer-processing that could not have been predicted by any process of technological forecasting (WP: 38–43; 1979: 175–7; 1992: 43–6). Bell uses Oettinger's term 'compunications' to describe this development. He contrasts a compunications system with an unintegrated communications system. Until the mid-twentieth century, communications were divided into two realms, the print realm of books, newspapers and mail, and the electrical realm of telephone, telegraph and radio. Compunications technology erases this distinction. Several component developments can be distinguished within this reorganization:

- the combination of telephone, computer networks and telecommunications into a single system;
- the displacement of paper processing by electronic media;
- an expansion of television transmission through cable, fibre-optics and satellites;
- localized computer networking and information retrieval; and
- expansions of the system into education, domestic contexts and remote and isolated arenas.

For Bell, much of this implies a new set of societal problems that centre on the control of the information that is transmitted and possibilities for informatic surveillance of individuals. This implication derives from an assumption that information can be centrally controlled by a small set of large mass media organizations.[6]

Two other developments are associated with the third technological revolution. The first is the new materials technology (1992: 32–40) that, if one is to believe Bell's alchemical enthusiasm, enables industries to fabricate any material to specification, although not independently of cost. Materials science is what Bell calls a 'knowledge expanded' discipline. By this he means that the fabrication of any material is possible precisely because that material can first be theorized. The new materials technology has widespread implications: it frees assembly from location near resource sites; it diminishes the powers of international commodities cartels; it can impoverish raw-materials-producing countries;

it increases energy efficiency; and it frees humanity from nature in a fundamental sense.

The second is the onset of automation in fabrication. In 1977 (WP: 43–5) Bell was relatively cautious about the arrival of automation, indicating that it would take at least 20 years to be fully accomplished. That caution was well-advised and might have been extended. Full robotic automation, the workerless factory, is still a relative rarity. However, computer technology and its informatic systems have wrought some remarkable changes. Bell was impressed by the diffusion of numerically controlled machine-tools but these have now more or less been superseded by computer numerically controlled machine tools. Of rather more importance, as Bell suggests, is the extent to which routine clerical work has been technologically upgraded with a consequent loss of employment and also the extent to which what he calls 'knowledge jobs' have been technologically empowered so that they can proceed much more rapidly and efficiently.

Taken together, all of these developments imply that society is moving into an information age or phase. In a familiar pattern, first established in COPIS, Bell moves to confirm this argument by examining secular trends in statistical indicators. Indeed, many of his empirical findings repeat or update those to be found in COPIS (see Chapter 6 for details). However, he is now able to distinguish the information sector from other service sectors (1979: 180–6). Drawing on Porot, he divides it into a primary information sector, industries that market information machines or information services, and a secondary information sector, sections of industries engaged in information and knowledge work but that are not normally measured as such because they enable the production of other commodities or services. In 1967 the primary sector accounted for 22 per cent of American GDP, but interestingly over 43 per cent of corporate profits, while the secondary sector accounted for a further 21 per cent. The composition of the work-force has changed similarly. If one divides the work-force into four employment sectors – agriculture, industry, services and information – by 1980 the last had become by far the largest, employing 47 per cent of American workers compared with 29 per cent in services and 23 per cent in industry. Bell has no hesitation in suggesting that the USA has entered the information age.

TIME AND SPACE

In WD (10; see Chapter 3) Bell discusses the way in which the discipline involved in industrial work is related to the invention of metric time. He shows that supervision and the measurement of efficiency only becomes possible when time can be divided into precise intervals. He also shows how the later invention of assembly-line manufacturing altered social organization in space because each requires a concentrated group of workers and 'a huge shed of space'. He can now move to examine the implications of industrial and post-industrial technology for the reorganization of time and space both inside and outside the sphere of work.

Pre-industrial societies were either space-bound or time-bound (WP: 62–3). The space-bound societies were the ancient empires held together by a military system of garrisons, while time-bound societies were usually smaller in scale but integrated by a common sense of ethnic or religious tradition. Because most people worked on land or water, time was measured by the exigencies of nature – the diurnal rhythm was established by the order of tasks that needed to be performed and the annual one by the rotation of the seasons. Industrial technology had several effects on this conception of time (1992: 17–18). The first effect was produced by increased speed: the accessibility of space expanded; distances shrunk; and time horizons extended. Electrical communications equally tended to enlarge social context, overcoming space and distance. Spatial constraints also declined as electric light made people less dependent on planetary rotation and gave them control of when they would work, eat or sleep. Similarly, as is noted above, the invention of synthetics provided an independence from nature that enabled fabrication to take place independently of resource sites and transportation costs.

Somewhat surprisingly, for Bell, the key technology that altered this construction of time was not the industrial factory but the railway (WP: 63–4). A railway network is a complex system that requires precision both in making connections and in avoiding collisions, especially given long lengths of single track. Although Bell possibly exaggerates when he says that this requires 'split-second timing', probably 'split-minute' timing would have done for a railroad system, it is nevertheless clear that unless such a network runs to a timetable it will be grossly inefficient, if not dangerous. The transcontinental railways of

North America and Eurasia also required new relativities to be established between local solar time and the abstract timetable. The standard time zones for North America were imposed by the railway companies themselves, rather than by governments, in 1875 and they were incorporated into the international time-zone system established at the Washington Meridian conference of 1885. Under the terms of that conference time was reconstituted out of local contexts into the common experience of global humanity.

These changes in transportation and communication have created national societies and have the potential to create a global society. Bell reserves the term 'national society' for nation-states in which none of the regions or social segments is isolated. The development of a national society means a loss of 'insulating space' so that any event will ramify throughout the entire system. This is felt particularly in politics. To illustrate, Bell compares the intense labour violence that occurred between 1870 and 1940 with the civil rights and anti-Vietnam war protests of the 1960s and 1970s (WP: 60–1). The former were isolated in single-industry towns and so had little impact on society at large while in the latter case small incidents could provoke the mobilization of vast numbers of people. The Vietnam war also provides Bell with his example of globalization because it demonstrated a capacity to extend military power across great distances. He does not mention that one of the reasons for a loss of domestic support for the war was the fact that its violence could not be insulated from television audiences.

Surprisingly, Bell says less about the impact of post-industrial than of industrial technologies on social constructions of space and time. He is certainly aware that space is now conceptualized as the entire planet and that time is frequently conceptualized as 'real time' (WP: 62–3). However, in the latter case he makes the error of indicating that all computer time is 'real time' when computers can only be described as processing in real time when they match the time-frame of the operator. Nevertheless, we can agree with Bell that the computer alters conceptions of time. It reduces time to minute proportions, down to picoseconds (10^{-12}) if one wishes. It also expands time in that it increases the number of tasks that fit into a given span.

The reorganization of space and time jointly created by industrial and post-industrial technologies has the following consequences (1979: 199–206; 1992: 48–52):

- *The location of cities.* In the pre-industrial world, cities were located in relation to natural transportation possibilities; in the industrial world, in relation to resource sites. In the post-industrial world cities are becoming disorganized and dispersed. New communications possibilities allow a decentralization of economic functions and population movements follow this dispersal.
- *Planning.* Large-scale regulation and co-ordination is likely to increase as the parts of human society become less insulated and the computer opens up possibilities for widespread information-gathering.
- *Centralization and privacy.* The capacity to store and retrieve large amounts of information poses threats to individual privacy.
- *The disruption of elites.* The knowledge elite is dispersing to the various situses within which information is organized.
- *A new geo-economic order.* The world order no longer depends on military security and power but on global capital flows and the distribution of manufacturing.

2013 AND ALL THAT

Despite all claims that forecasting can only propose the questions that will need to be answered and the limits within which they can be answered, Bell cannot resist attempting a little futurology (WP: 210–27; 1987). The reservations are still there of course:

> Though an effort at forecasting, it is still a cautionary tale in the face of the technological 'gee-whiz' and the kind of 'future schlock' that has us hurtling into the future without a sense of the recalcitrances of people and the constraints of institutions that create turbulences in the winds of change'. [1987: 4–5]

Indeed, he insists that it is not an effort to predict the future but only to provide a framework for analysis. He chooses the date 2013 for no other apparent reason than 'that it is sufficiently different in time to transcend immediate and particular issues' (1987: 1). The only basis for the choice of date might be that 1987, the publication date of the 'The world and the United States in 2013', is thirteen short of the century but, in any event,

Bell makes no forecast of the date at which any particular development might occur.

Bell begins by addressing structural change at the global level. The major possibility here is a shift in economic power from the North Atlantic to the Pacific rim and a consequent shift in political and military power. Speculatively, Bell even canvasses the possibility of a Eurasian bloc stretching from Germany to China, if Russia can put its economic and political house in order. This shift will be matched by a more profound one that will involve the constitution of a 'new international division of labour'. The previous core economies will be post-industrialized, concentrating on flexible manufacturing and informatic industries. Routine manufacturing is shifting to the low-labour-cost economies of the 'Third World'. Thus, the centres of manufacturing are multiplying but so too are the centres of finance so that capital is becoming internationalized. The third key structural change that accompanies these is the third technological revolution, as discussed above. This will have the effect of eliminating the constraints of geography. Associated with this technological shift will be the conquest of new frontiers, the colonization of the macro-frontier of space and the manipulation of the micro-frontier of biotechnology. The latter will be the arena, Bell forecasts, of the fourth technological revolution.

One of Bell's cautions in social forecasting is that one should not merely project trends and construct frameworks but that one should identify 'undertows', currents that threaten to disrupt or reverse what he views as the steady march of social progress. In a slide into technological determinism he admits that, 'the thrust [of the argument] has tended to be – cautiously – on the positive side, because of the underlying technological possibilities' (1987: 13). He identifies two particular structural threats. The first is the fragmentation of nation-states in the face of intractable problems. He captures the source of the problem in a sentence now famous among theorists of globalization: 'the national state has become too small for the big problems in life, and too big for the small problems' (WP: 225, italics deleted; 1987: 13–14, with stylistic variation). By this he means that the nation-state is being torn apart by its incapacity to control international economic effects and an inability to respond to local needs. The nation-state is fragmenting in two directions (WP: 225–6). First, ethnic minorities are pushing towards geographical fragmentation into ethnically homogeneous segments (the former nation-states of the Soviet

Union, Yugoslavia and Czechoslovakia are relevant examples). Second, 'organized corporate groups' (i.e. unions and professional associations) are seeking exemption from responsibilities for the well-being of fellow citizens by making excessive income demands that will tend to exacerbate inflation. The response in the middle class is a tax revolt that may 'bankrupt' the state.

Bell's second 'time bomb' is demography, not absolute population growth but the concentration of populations in large cities. In the Third World, in particular, this will create serious problems at the level of social services and economic infrastructure. The social-services problem is likely to be exacerbated by the disproportionate age structure of the population which is now creating huge educational demands and will, by 2013, create major demands for meaningful employment. It may come as a surprise to learn that Bell discounts resource shortages as a possible time bomb: commodities are substitutable and can be replaced by synthetics; food surpluses are high and famines are now caused mainly by political mismanagement; and energy conservation appears to be increasingly effective. Bell makes no mention of issues of environmental pollution or global warming.

Bell can now turn to the USA. He forecasts a framework of five elements for the year 2013 (1987: 20–9):

- a bi-coastal economy resulting from post-industrial expansion and the decline of the 'rust belt' and of labour-intensive agriculture;
- a central government that is ineffective in providing services;
- a population that is ageing and increasingly non-white/non-Anglo;
- an increasing number of single-parent families;
- a four-tier class structure defined by education (professional and managerial upper middle class, 25 per cent; technical and administrative middle class, 35 per cent; personal service class, 25 per cent; underclass 15 per cent) involving the break-up of the traditional middle class and the consequent emergence of a new politics based on gender, generation, region, race and ethnicity.

The key problem that American society needs to solve is the problem of 'mismatch of scale' indicated in the above quotation about the nation-state (WP: 214–221). The state is in a double bind in so far as it must both steer the system in the direction of increased capital accumulation and meet the consumption demands of its citizens. In meeting both of these obligations it has typically resorted to debt financing and the debt, in the USA as elsewhere, is becoming all-consuming and unmanageable. The problem will be exacerbated by the reduction in the tax base caused by increasing dependency ratios in the population.

The curious feature of this forecast is the disjunction between the projected condition of the world in 2013 and that of the USA. The world is claimed to be in a state of post-industrialization and technological advance, tempered only by the threat of the fragmentation of the nation-state which some might view as not too value-negative anyway, while the USA is besieged by problems that threaten to rip it apart. Bell has written frequently of American exceptionalism, the notion that America is a unique type of society (EI: 95–103; WP 245–72; 1989). He fears that the exceptionalism that derived from a non-ideologized polity is now disappearing and that America will become as politically divided as any other society. Perhaps this version needs to be recast in the light of his forecasts for 2013. American exceptionalism, as Bell confides, is the outcome of technological and economic global dominance so that the USA could afford both to accumulate capital and to fund consumption. If American industry is in relative decline in global terms then the maintenance of an individualized but amicable civil society might no longer be possible. Politics might have become the 'cockpit of society', not because knowledge rules but because capital now rules from another part of the world.

CONCLUSION

It would not cast too much of an aspersion on Daniel Bell to describe him as a 'technology freak'. Certainly, he writes lengthily, enthusiastically and knowledgeably about technological developments. He is particularly interested in the cutting edge, in such issues as materials science, photo-optics and miniaturization. The conjunction between this interest in technology and the commitment to forecasting must lead us to the question of whether Bell is a technological determinist. On three grounds the answer must be negative. First, in his discussions of technological forecasting he always insists that technological development is the product of its social context. Second, in engaging in forecasts about technology and society he is always careful to do no more than claim that technology sets the limits for social possibilities. Technology causes problems that must be solved at the social and political levels. However, there is no ineluctable link between any techno-logical development and any social one and he would presumably be more sanguine about social forecasting if there were. Third, he also insists that the new technologies of the post-industrial era are intellectual rather than physical and that such technologies can only be constructed and used in social contexts. If Bell's enthusiasm about technological developments sometimes gets the better of him, as when he associates historical shifts in technology with historical shifts in social structure, he nevertheless manages to return to these fundamentals.

The frustrating paradox of futurology is that while the future is contained in the present it is never clear which elements of the present are likely to be salient. Bell is probably correct in suggest-ing that this is where sociology can make its most important contribution, that is, not in projecting trend lines but in identifying those structural components of the present on which we should concentrate. This is presumably why many observers accuse him of being unable to make up his mind about whether post-indus-trial society has arrived, is coming or is coming-into-being (see Chapter 6). Certainly, that particular framework is the universal central theme of his forecasting – the fragmentary materials on the information age and the third technological revolution are but pendants to this central idea. The exception is the '2013' material (WP: 210–27; 1987) which genuinely seeks to forecast a set of outcomes. The problem is that it is not constructed around any identifiable social framework but rather appears as a list of speculations about the future based precisely on a projection of trends. It needs to be stressed that these speculations are intelligent, interesting and useful and that they are occasionally sociologically informed. But they are not careful and deliberative theoretical constructions and, as such, do not conform with the criteria Bell himself frequently sets out for proper forecasting. They have the character of intelligent journalism, with all the capacity for the provocative stimulation of debate that this description implies, as well as a flimsy theoretical foundation.

One such area of debate might be the grounds for the decline of American predominance (and exceptionalism). We have seen that Bell locates this development in the theorized context of a double bind or contradiction that bears considerable similarity to an argument mounted by Offe (1984). In so doing, Bell expresses the standard fears of the middle-class conservative, that is, that inflation is getting out of hand, that people want too much, and that debts are getting too big to repay. The difficulty is that the inflationary cycle and the industrial decline that have afflicted the USA may be attributable to entirely different causes to those adduced by Bell. Inflation was the direct consequence of deliberate and ideologically motivated government policy in the 1980s that involved massive spending, not on welfare, but on defence and on tax-cuts that were intended to cultivate corporate and middle-class political support.[7] Industrial decline was due to the abject failure on the part of managers of American corporations to recognize the efficiencies that lay in flexible manufacturing and in engaging workers in a shared enterprise. It is curious that Bell should so frequently and heavily stress the importance of human agency and insist that politics is the cockpit of society but in the end resort to, in Australian terms, 'union bashing' and the stigmatization of 'welfare bludgers' as his explanation for inflation.

That said, other sociologists can only applaud Bell's willingness to go on the public record with his informed speculations. Their accessibility provides a profile to the discipline that will never be accomplished either by the detailed mathematical manipulation of trivia or by the abstruse theoretical argument that is sociology's usual stock-in-trade. But the best last words said in defence of Bell are perhaps his own:

> A disciplined effort to identify structural changes – in the face of the overwhelming weight of political and cultural imponderables, let alone the irrational tides of hatred and anger – leads one to a sense of the futility of such 'rational' efforts. It is like holding a small candle in a hurricane to see if there are any paths ahead and how to go forth. But if one cannot light and hold even a small candle, then there is only darkness before us. [1987: 31]

9

Dazzling the Goyim

International Sociology, which is the lead journal of the International Sociological Association and is distributed to all its members, occasionally publishes short biographies or 'portraits' of leading figures in the discipline. As I became interested in the work of Daniel Bell it seemed appropriate and overdue that his portrait should also appear in the journal, and so I offered to write one. The editors declined on the grounds that Bell was much too well-known a figure to need to be introduced to the members of the ISA and asked whether there was perhaps some rising Australian sociologist who might benefit from such exposure.[1] The simple fact is that Bell is read throughout sociology, by theoreticians at the cutting edge, by empiricists seeking a framework that will lend cogency to their findings, by Marxists in search of the opponent, by new cultural theorists, and by students seeking a relatively accessible entrée to an understanding of contemporary social change. And, as those editors well knew, he is read by sociologists throughout the world.

For some sociologists such a reputation would be enough; for most it is beyond their wildest imaginings. Bell is important not merely because he is read widely but because he has an unusual capacity to bridge academic and public discourse so that he finds respect and admiration not only among colleagues but also in the elite and the middle mass. Bell fulfils the role of the *Schriftsteller*, the public intellectual *par excellence*. Other sociologists have also fulfilled such a role including, in Bell's own generation, David Riesman, Nathan Glazer and C. Wright Mills, and in the contemporary context one can think of such figures as Amitai Etzioni and Ulrich Beck, but none is as effective or as famous as Bell. The reason may simply be that Bell is entirely courageous and straightforward. When he develops an idea that he believes in he does not fall victim to false modesty, a character trait to which he would never admit, but rather touts it in the intellectual market place. If that requires replicated publication he will cut and paste and find another outlet. If people do not listen or agree or understand he does not elaborate but bludgeons them with repetition. If people write to him or criticize him in print, he writes reams in response. He goes out of his way to grant interviews. Bell's fame is not an accident but a reflexive, self-conscious, Franklinian effort to compose the self that combines outstanding talent, voluminous reading, a supportive intellectual circle and a capacity for self-salesmanship. Perhaps Bell would not be too unhappy if the account he himself gives for Benjamin Franklin's business success was also given for his own academic success:

> [A]ll this was partly cunning, and perhaps even deceit. While Franklin was thrifty and industrious, his success like that of many a good Yankee, came from his capacity to make influential friends, an uncanny ability to advertise himself, and the charm and wit reflected in the person and his writing'. [CCC: 58]

In this concluding chapter we consider Bell's influence in the public and the academic arenas. In the former case, because it has been addressed so often, the key question must be whether Bell is a neo-conservative. In the latter, the problem might be to explain Bell's influence. The chapter closes with a forecast, that of whether Bell will in the future be regarded as a defining, classical figure or a mere disciplinary eccentricity – can he be a Mead rather than a Sorokin, a Lazarsfeld rather than a Lundberg?

THE PUBLIC IMAGE

For many there is no doubt that the sociological image that Bell presents to the public is neo-conservative. It is seen as denying the existence of arbitrary power and reacting against new cultural and political movements in a panic fear of anarchy and nihilism. Habermas (1983), for example, is entirely comfortable in locating Bell at what he calls the productive centre of American neo-conservatism. For him, anyone associated with the American Committee for Cultural Freedom, as Bell was, embraces the two central neo-conservative principles of anti-communism and anti-populism. Similarly, O'Neill (1988) reads Bell's analysis of culture as a neoconservative lament about the loss of tradition in the face of hedonism and postmodernism. For Wald (1987: 353), Bell appears as a minor ideologue of the neo-conservative movement although a divergent within it.[2] Perhaps the most convincing claim is made by Steinfels:

> To a large extent, Bell has been labelled a neoconserva-tive because he runs with the neoconservatives. Kristol is an old friend, whom Bell repeatedly cites as such. His references to Kristol ... to Seymour Martin Lipset, a collaborator on several projects, to Samuel P. Huntington, a colleague at Harvard, to Herman Kahn, and to other neoconservatives almost always express agreement. If he takes exception to some of their views the difference has not been such as to provoke him to public criticism. [1979: 165]

As we have seen, Bell rejects the label because it denies the complexity of his own value-commitments and their divergences from the views of confessed neo-conservatives. He insists also on his right to maintain friendships with such individuals as Kristol, with whose views he frequently disagrees. Any rejection of friend-ship and common experience on the basis of another's political or religious commitments would, for Bell, be morally repugnant. Rather, to Wald's disgust and to the surprise of almost everyone else, Bell insists that he is still a socialist, if only in the area of economics. While one might question the possibility of being a non-political socialist, the issue of whether Bell's self-description in tripartite terms (socialist in economics, liberal in politics, con-servative in culture; see Chapter 1) is accurate might provide a rather more interesting exploration.

The claim to being a socialist in economics involves a commitment to the provision of a minimum material standard of living especially, for example, in the area of health-care provision. It specifically precludes statist intervention (though how socialist objectives can be achieved without it is unclear) and worker ownership of the means of production. The problem is that this is not all that a socialist might say about the economic realm. A socialist would, almost certainly, be critical about the distribution of capital ownership and the power that it confers. Bell quite clearly is not: class evils disappeared with the break-up of family capitalism; economic privilege does not reproduce itself; and contemporary corporations, once bureaucracies, are becoming collegial communities in the post-industrial society. These arguments are debateable, but their accuracy is not the issue here. Rather, what is certain, is that one cannot simultaneously be a socialist and cleave to them. Bell's critique of the economic sphere tends to the view that it is bureaucratized and over-regulated, that it suppresses individual freedom and creativity, rather than to the view that it is exploitative. All this suggests that in the economic sphere Bell is liberal (in the American sense of stressing individual liberty plus welfare) rather than socialist. But there is also a clear conservative streak in so far as he remains blind to the possibilities of corporate power. In economic terms, he would be quite comfortable in either of the mainstream American parties, neither of which could remotely be described as socialist.

The claim to political liberalism is more convincing. Bell makes explicit statements consistent with Jeffersonian democracy about individual rights, small government (notwithstanding a grudging approval for the New Deal) and the sanctity of the private sphere. Indeed, he believes passionately in the state as a constitutional sphere where the rules are the only reality. Yet, as noted in Chapter 4, he adopts a strikingly illiberal pose in suggesting that the public household needs to be the arbiter of justice, meritocracy and individual economic minimums precisely because the market is inadequate to make such allocations. The public household can be nothing but the state. Indeed, in COPIS he indicates approvingly that such a development is, in fact, occurring insofar as politics is becoming the cockpit of society. Here politics is not a source of last-resort interventions but rather an arena within which primary steering, e.g. planning, takes place.

Very few would disagree with Bell that he is a conservative in culture, although it must be stressed that his position is elitist and traditionalist rather than succumbing to the insistence on economic rationalism that is at the heart of neo-conservatism. He clearly does not believe that the value of cultural objects should be determined by the market. The problem rather lies in his insistence that the three realms are independent. If he wants a return to authoritative standards in culture then there must be a source of such standards, and its only possibility is an illiberal state. If he wants to divert individual preferences away from self-gratification and towards tradition, quality and morality this would entail intervention in the private sphere. Moreover, his insistence that culture does indeed frame preferences implies that an instaurative return to religion of the type he envisages can only result in an anti-modernizing hierocratic state of the type found in Iran or desired by the right wing of Israeli politics. Bell would deplore such a development.

There can be little doubt of the genuine value-implications of Bell's sociology. He is not a neo-conservative but neither is he remotely a socialist nor much of a liberal. Despite all interest in the future possibilities of technology and post-industrialism Bell is an old-fashioned, traditionalistic, elitist conservative. He believes in the sanctity of the family and the private sphere, the constitution of the USA, authoritative standards in culture, the exposure of the young to the Western intellectual tradition, responsibility to the community, and religious morality. He is opposed to anarchy and nihilism, extremism, self-gratification, anti-nomianism, affirmative action, the recognition of the special disadvantages of women and racial minorities, economic individualism, and regulation. He might be guilty of nostalgia but not of inhumanity.

THE SOCIOLOGICAL CONTRIBUTION

Bell's central legacy to sociology is the role he played in fracturing the holistic hegemony, the two variants of the dominant ideology thesis (see Abercrombie, Hill and Turner 1980) at the level of general theory. The theory of the three realms is by no means fully developed but it does provide a conceptual map of the terrain over which sociology stakes its intellectual claim. Theoretical sociology as it is currently practised bears a much greater resemblance to Bell than it does to Marx or Parsons.

One of Bell's greatest strengths is his ability to sense shifts in the *Zeitgeist*, to locate them within the Western tradition and to recast them in a provocative and stimulating way. If one had to select the biggest of the big ideas then it would have to be that of the post-industrial society, the primary example of this capacity and the idea that will always be associated with his name. As we saw in Chapter 6, the idea got away from him and entered the collective wisdom almost before he had finished formulating it.

We are now accustomed to theories of New Times. As Bell, somewhat hypocritically wails, 'everything is now either Post or "End of . . ." Is there not anywhere to go?' (Bell to Waters 3/1/94). His was the first full-blown theory of the New Times and, in a genetic as much as in a generational sense, it is the grandaddy of them all. Although examples that locate Bell in the avant-garde of contemporary theory abound in this book, we can here summarize the most important ones.[3]

- The end-of-ideology thesis anticipates many recent theories of 'new' or post-materialist politics (e.g. Inglehart 1990) because it specifies that politics will be detached from class milieux and refocused on values and lifestyles. Bell's analysis is not as sanguine as many of those that succeed it. In fact, he anticipates the breakdown of the coalitions that underpin the American two-party system in favour of a politics that emphasizes transitory commitment and disturbing upswells of opinion and manifestation. Nevertheless, the politics envisaged by the public-household argument is a politics of multiple status- and lifestyle-claimants and not a politics of stable class formations.
- In WD Bell argues that industrialization reorganized human conceptions of time and space in the direction of generality and metricity. This anticipates a similar proposal made by McLuhan (1964) that was subsequently taken up by Giddens (1991) and, in linking time-metrication to issues of work discipline, also prefigures a central component of Foucault's surveillance thesis (1979). Bell returns to the themes of time and space at several points. The idea of the 'eclipse of distance' in modernist cultural expression in which the stress is on simultaneity, impact, sensation and immediacy resonates closely with Harvey's analysis (1988) of the postmodern sensibility. And, although written at about the same time, Bell's appraisal of the impact of transportation and communications technology on social constructions of space and time is very similar to those of Harvey (1988) and Giddens (1991).
- The key contribution of CCC is an analysis of postmodernism

written long before that topic became fashionable. Bell's interpretation is, of course, fundamentally different from that of say Harvey (1988), Lash and Urry (1987) or Crook, Pakulski and Waters (1992): Harvey locates the postmodern sensibility in the collapse of time and space; Lash and Urry link postmodern culture to a rising class; while Crook et al. see the emergence of what they call 'postculture' as part of widespread ironic reversal of prevailing social trends. As we have seen, Bell views postmodernism as an extreme, perhaps unintended development of modernism. Nevertheless, each of these three arguments draws on Bell's view that postmodernism involves the disruption and involution of tradition and the cultivation of a mobile, self-gratifying psyche.

- CCC also anticipates contemporary theories of 'detraditionalization' (Beck 1992; Giddens 1991) that propose that late modernity involves a recasting of modernization as 'reflexive modernization'. Here individuals are no longer the product of social situations but are deliberately self-composing in a calculus that compares the self with an idealized goal structure derived from the mass media and expert systems. The apposite idea in Bell is that of *discretionary social behaviour* (see Chapter 7) that specifies that behaviour patterns are increasingly attributable to the idiosyncratic aspects of individuals rather than to their social location, especially in class structures.

- One of Bell's minor papers (1987) even anticipates contemporary theories of globalization (e.g. Featherstone 1990; Robertson 1992; Waters 1995). Indeed, his pithy epigram about the nation-state becoming too small for the big problems and too large for the small ones has become one of the most quoted within that thematic area.

- Perhaps the only one of the New Times theories that Bell failed to anticipate was that which specified the direction of change as post-Fordism or 'flexible specialization' (e.g. Harvey 1988; Kern and Schumann 1984; Piore and Sabel 1984). For Bell, there is no hope that the sphere of work can be anything other than bureaucratized and alienating. This is a curious anomaly given his interest in the social effects of technology.

- However, his theory of post-industrialization has been appropriated directly in several instances. Two are particularly important. Lyotard's influential analysis of the postmodern condition (1984) draws directly on Bell in so far as he claims that society is moving into a post-industrial age and culture into a postmodern age. However, in Lyotard, the two operate in tandem rather than in contradiction. Post-industrial developments see the commodification of knowledge through the application of new technologies. Increasingly, 'performativity', the capacity to deliver outputs at the lowest cost, replaces truth as the yardstick of knowledge. Culture therefore dissolves into a series of localized and flexible networks of language games and loses its capacity to attract generalized commitment. Lash and Urry's recent specification of reflexive accumulation (1994) also draws directly on Bell. Post-industrialization proliferates cognitive signs, symbols that represent information. These signs become the central components of production, displacing material components. Expert services and their signification are the crucial factor in the success of contemporary production systems.

Bell would put himself at some distance from other New Times theories. The caveats he places on the post-industrial society thesis in which, nomenclature notwithstanding, he is not theorizing the emergence of a post-industrial *society* but only a post-industrial, techno-economic structure, and his insistence that postmodernism is only an extreme extension of modernism confirm this view. But, like it or not, this is exactly where his work has been most influential. Paradoxically, those who reject the notion of New Times in proposing that the current context is best theorized as high modernity or late capitalism (e.g. Giddens 1991; Habermas 1981; Jameson 1984) would find least in common with Bell[4]. The original concepts of post-industrialism and postmodernism that Bell developed have taken on a life of their own. They now centre a galaxy of theories that propose that a historical phase-shift is under way. They could not be more influential, but it is unlikely that their author would subscribe to the ways in which they are now employed.

A NEW CLASSIC?

In the second half of the twentieth century, sociology has thrown up two figures that can undeniably stand alongside the founding parents of its classical period. They are Talcott Parsons and Jürgen Habermas. While a fair appraisal of Bell would not unequivocally put him in the same league he would certainly have a claim to be at the head of the next small group to be considered.[5]

If Bell does have a lasting influence, and the current indications are that he will, it will be for two reasons. First, his big ideas have been put forward with such courage and enthusiasm that they have permeated both the sociological and the popular consciousness. Second, his work is so full of ideas and formulations, many of them loose and slippery, others inconsistent and even contradictory, but all supported by a supreme intellect and a restless enthusiasm for ideas, that it is intensively seminal and provocative. Elsewhere this book has drawn parallels between Bell and Weber in this respect. Bell offers a rich lode for future scholars to refine. And as Steinfels says: 'One need not adhere to Bell's ideological outlook or his policy preferences to find in his work a rich mine of useful analyses and thoughtful "agendas" of social issues' (1979: 185).

Perhaps we can leave it to Steinfels to sum Bell up:

> Bell's is a brittle kind of brilliance. Like the society he analyses it takes everything as raw material and processes it swiftly. . . . There is little serenity in this whirligig of information and ideas. Bell's mind is a fascinating place to visit but obviously it would be demanding to live there. Implicit in this strenuous brilliance is a notion of excellence . . . that does not look back to an unrealizable past but seeks its discipline and even grandeur in the very press of modern capitalism . . . but that does not really offer any alternative but to ride the tiger of our fragmented and contradictory capitalism . . . with an acute awareness of its fearful symmetry and constant recollection of the heritage that this ride endangers. [1979: 186–7].

Put more simply, Bell's work is an excellent read. Sociology, and American sociology in particular, would have been acutely impoverished had not the prodigal son returned to dazzle us with his brilliance.

Notes

1 RETURN OF A PRODIGAL SON

[1] Kadushin does not reveal who is the single most influential American intellectual.

[2] The reader need not be concerned that this estimate is Amerocentric. While he would not be regarded as a public intellectual anywhere else, he has a formidable reputation. His books sell very widely outside sociological circles throughout the world, having been published in multiple translations. In his retirement Bell also established himself as a public figure in East Asia through the medium of journalism.

[3] Merton is the only other sociologist in Kadushin's list to be included in this series so far.

[4] For Bell's major works I am using a referencing system that relies on the initials of the book. See the reference list at the end of this book for full details. The four main sources are *The End of Ideology* (EI), *The Winding Passage* (WP), *The Coming of Post-Industrial Society* (COPIS) and *The Cultural Contradictions of Capitalism* (CCC).

[5] This section is based on: Simons (1988: 56–72); Bell's curriculum vitae; the prefaces to WP and CCC; and interviews I held with Mr Bell in November 1993.

[6] Finkelstein later moved to England, changed his name to Finlay, became a Fellow of Jesus College, Cambridge, then Master of Darwin College, and eventually was knighted.

[7] Bell explains: 'Before the war and even in the early years of the war there was never any expectation that you'd get an academic job. This was true of almost everybody I knew at the time. It simply wasn't there' (Simons 1988: 72). On the other hand, Bell was without a higher degree or direct experience of research and scholarship. He was 20 years old with a BA in ancient history from a non-Ivy League school. He would not have appeared to be much of a catch.

[8] It is fortunate indeed that Bell worked in the USA and not, say, Australia. The latter academic system does not offer anything like those four good reasons. Sociology would otherwise have lost a great talent.

[9] Bell begins his autobiographical preface to WP with a paraphrase of the opening lines of Dante's *Paradiso*: 'These are the essays of a prodigal son. They are essays written in my middle years, midway in the journey of our life, in that dark wood, seeking a return to the straight way of my ancestors' (WP: xvii).

[10] Bell took leave from *Fortune* in 1956–7 and, for a while, worked full-time in Paris as the seminar organizer for the Congress.

[11] For Bell's generational list of members see WP: 127–9. The overlap between this list and Kadushin's list of 70 is very revealing. Bell's list accounts for nine of the top ten and seven of the next ten but only 17 of the next 50. Either the New York circle was extraordinarily influential or there was a tight exchange of votes between them or, most likely, both.

[12] He writes: 'I recently received a long essay on my "cultural" views from a young man of the conservative right, which praises me mightily for my "profound" views. Save me from my friends.' (Bell to Waters 3/1/94).

[13] It is clear that he regarded himself as a counterweight to the arch-neo-conservative, Kristol: 'When I stepped down as co-editor of *The Public Interest* Nat [Glazer] took my place on the balance wheel of the magazine' (WP: xxx).

2 THE THREE REALMS

[1] Bell must be referring here to contemporary Western society. Elsewhere he offers two possibilities for the sources of social order, although he also makes explicit the origin of the contractualist position he espouses: 'Every society (to paraphrase Rousseau) is held together by coercion – army, militia, police – or by a moral order, the willingness of individuals to respect each other and to respect the rules of common law.' (CCC: 154).

[2] This argument stands against prevailing wisdom about the prevalence of just such value-patterns in Scandinavia, postwar Germany, Australasia, and perhaps even Japan.

[3] For all his alleged conservatism Bell would almost certainly want to disassociate himself from such statements as the one made by the British political leader, Margaret Thatcher: 'There is no such thing as society, only individuals and families struggling to get by.' On the other hand, Bell might endorse Thatcher's attempt to restore those individualistic bourgeois values of which he also regrets the passing.

[4] I put this point to Daniel Bell in an interview in November 1993. He replied that it was 'a good question'.

3 LABOUR AND CAPITAL

[1] He regards Schumpeter as a model economist in these terms.

[2] Like Foucault (1979) he invokes the example of Bentham's panoptical model prison and also draws an analogy between the prison and the factory (WD: 1–3).

[3] Although Bell's analyses might sometimes be suspect, his capacity to anticipate future social and intellectual developments is occasionally quite breathtaking. WD was written in 1956, yet he was already anticipating post-Fordist and flexible specialization developments and the literature that surrounds them. In writing about the cost limitations of inflexible, single-product, automated technology he says: 'the adoption of these expensive machines will only delay the coming of the flexible automatic machines, capable of turning out a wide variety of products, and producing a true machine revolution.' (WD: 49).

[4] Bell is wrong in supposing that productivity provides limits to the yields that can be returned to labour by collective

bargaining. Collective bargaining is a distributional process that divides surplus between claimants. It can determine the share of surplus received by wage-earners relative to the shares that go to reinvestment, taxes, executive salaries, dividends, managerial perquisites, stock options, and so on.

[5] Bell is critical not only of economizing as a general social process but also of the analytic possibilities that are provided by the discipline of economics (see CET; DHB).

[6] One implication for Bell is that each of these constituencies should be represented on Boards of Directors (COPIS: 296).

[7] Much of the opening part of this section is based on an unpublished paper developed for teaching purposes called 'Marx and the Concept of Class' that Mr Bell made available.

[8] Elsewhere, Bell includes managerial power under skill: 'A class system defines the mode of gaining wealth and privilege in a society. (This mode can be land [real property], corporate title ['fictitious' property], skill [technical or managerial], mercenaries [*condottori*], or direct political allocation [party, bureaucracy, or army], and this class system has to be legitimated, in legal forms, in order to assure its continuity)' (EI: 66; original italics).

[9] Bell gives a different, more systemic definition of class in COPIS (361; italics deleted): 'Class denotes not a specific group of persons but a system that has institutionalized the ground rules for acquiring, holding, and transferring differential power and its attendant privileges.'

[10] For fuller details of the stratification system in post-industrial society see Chapter 6.

[11] I must confess to a certain bias in favour of the alternative position suggested. It is the line I take in my own work on stratification (see e.g. Waters 1994).

4 THE EXHAUSTION OF POLITICAL EXTREMISM

[1] In American politics the term 'liberal' tends to imply tolerance of and support for non-productive status-groups (racial and ethnic minorities, women, sexual preference minorities, etc.) whereas in Britannic contexts it implies a commitment to the market as a distributive system.

[2] Bell published his original piece on American exceptionalism (WP: 245–71) in 1975. Since then the re-alignment he

predicted has come about, at least partially, and not only in the USA. The significant development was the splitting of the working-class vote in both the USA and Britain, the affluent sections of which became, respectively, 'Reagan Democrats' and 'working-class Tories'. The Democrats also lost their Southern conservative, 'Dixiecrat' support to the Republicans.

[3] He is also suggesting that his critics should address the particular argument that he offers rather than their own particular interpretation of his title.

[4] The extent to which Bell is a polemicist can be inspected in the titles of the various contributions to the volume edited by Waxman (1968). Aron, Shils and Lipset each add a question mark to their titles. For Bell, there is no question about the issue.

[5] The second theoretical aspect of the thesis (1990a) focuses entirely on Marxist ideology, seeking to show that it fails as an ideology because it fails as a theory of the social determination of ideas.

[6] In a later, possibly more considered statement, he defines ideology in the following way: 'the mobilization of ideas to commit people to action, and to justify those ideas by a teleology or a normative criterion' (1990a: 1).

[7] He repeats this self-misreading in a recent paper in the *Berkeley Journal of Sociology*: '*The End of Ideology* was a prognosis of the disintegration of Marxism as a faith system, but it did not say that "all" ideology was finished.' (1990a: 1) This must be a dissimulative formulation because in EI Bell certainly does argue that all ideology is finished in the West, as the quotations given here show. Indeed, he does not confine himself entirely to the West. As early as 1976 he was asking: 'would one dispute the end of ideology in the Soviet Union?' (CCC: 244).

[8] Although the general idea is extremely useful, the familistic terminology may be misleading. Economic exchanges in families operate ideally in terms of positive reciprocity while markets operate in terms of negative reciprocity. The most widely accepted norm of exchange in the state is that reciprocity should be neutral. To distinguish politically based economic exchanges from kinship-based economic exchanges Bell might have been advised to use a more distinctive terminology that nevertheless retained connotations of the

common good. Perhaps a modification of Parsons' term 'societal community' to read 'public community' would have sufficed. The formulation bears some similarity to Habermas' 'public sphere of the lifeworld' (1984; 1987) although Habermas would not see this as an economic arena. Nevertheless, Habermas' call for a reconstruction of that sphere bears a considerable resemblance to Bell's call for the institutionalization of the public household.

[9] This formulation owes something to the subtitle of Mandeville's famous fable (1924) that reads, 'or, Private Vices, Publick Benefits'.

5 AN EXCURSION INTO EDUCATION

[1] In Ivy League universities the undergraduate wing of the organization is often called the 'college'.

[2] The Union of Soviet Socialist Republics, a federated socialist state centred on Russia but now dismembered.

[3] Here Bell makes explicit the parallel with capitalist labour processes, comparing adolescent drop-out patterns with similar responses to discipline by the nineteenth-century working class in the forms of wildcat strikes and machine-breaking.

[4] Bell's language is irrevocably and, by current standards, unacceptably sexist. Workers are always 'men' and humanity is always 'man'. The language is even sexist when not required by convention, e.g. college students appear always to be 'boys' (RGE: 143).

[5] For all that he engages in attempted prediction and forecasting, Bell is firmly committed to the view that the future is rendered unpredictable by complexity, charisma and unforeseeable events.

6 THE POST-INDUSTRIAL SOCIETY

[1] Bell refers to *Old Worlds for New: A Study of the Post-Industrial State*. Here, Penty conceptualizes the post-industrial state as a primitive communist or anarchist utopia of small artisanal workshops (COPIS: 37n). Penty had earlier published a volume of essays with Ananda K. Coomaraswamy entitled *Essays in Post-Industrialism: A Symposium of Prophecy on the Future Society* (1914) and he also published

a subsequent monograph called simply *Post-Industrialism* (1922) (Rose 1991: 21–4).

[2] Touraine (1977) later protests that he can get no credit for the conceptualization against Bell. However, this is not surprising because he only uses the term as the title for his book. It does not appear at all in the text where he prefers the term, 'the programmed society'. Touraine's choice of title therefore leaves an impression of opportunism.

[3] Elsewhere (COPIS: 13), he lists engineers with scientists and technocrats among 'the hierophants of the new [post-industrial] society'.

[4] This is the closest thing Bell provides to a formal definition of 'post-industrial society' that I can find. Leibowitz (1985: 176) estimates that there are nine definitions in COPIS but this may be both an over- and an underestimate. Bell does not formally define the concept at all but the descriptions of the post-industrial society are multiple. Pahl (1975: 347) counts over fifty different uses of the term.

[5] Here Bell slips into a substantive description of the growth of these groups in the USA rather than giving ideal-typical details. He is quite clear that dominance does not translate into rule (interview 9/11/94) so it is unclear what he means by 'pre-eminence'.

[6] Bell's view can be contrasted with that of Beck (1990) who argues that risk in contemporary society is inherently incalculable and uncontrollable.

[7] The few lines in this foreword represent one of the rare occasions on which Bell mentions women at all. For another, see COPIS: 146.

[8] The unionization rate declined very rapidly in the USA during the 1980s, after Bell wrote COPIS. By the end of the decade it had reached 15 per cent (Crook, Pakulski and Waters 1992: 134n).

[9] Bell gives an extensive discussion of the way in which the expansion of outputs within a closed system follows a sigmoid or ∫ curve (COPIS: 179–85). The limits are reached at the top of the curve. Branching involves the multiplication and overlapping of ∫ curves.

[10] The use of proportions can be misleading. For example, a Third-World society with a small GDP and a commitment to educating its population might well spend a high pro-

portion in that area but this would scarcely qualify it as a 'knowledge society'.

[11] Bell defines class thus: 'Class, in the final sense, denotes not a specific group of persons but a system that has institutionalized the ground rules for acquiring, holding, and transferring differential power and its attendant privileges' [COPIS: 361].

[12] Bell introduces these issues to indicate that the area of co-ordination is one of the new scarcities of post-industrial society, along with information, and time (COPIS: 466–74).

[13] Appropriately he also regrets being the beneficiary of any fashion for an interest in social change, any association with what he calls 'future schlock' (COPIS: xi).

7 THE CONTRADICTIONS OF CULTURE

[1] Bell fails here to foresee that the expansion and differentiation of consumption markets would eventually force changes in the economic realm in the direction of flexible specialization (see Crook, Pakulski and Waters 1992: 167–96; c.f. Bell 1993).

[2] Bell's insistence on the recursive nature of cultural development, and indeed his use of the Italian word, can probably be traced to Vico (1984: 397–415).

[3] This section draws on an unpublished set of notes written in the early 1980s entitled 'Cultural Universals and a Universal Culture' supplied by Mr Bell.

[4] The list appears to be the product of personal reflection rather than being grounded in any systematic theoretical exercise. Bell does not make clear why these elements are central to the human predicament as opposed to say, how people find meaning in the face of injustice, inequality or interpersonal violence, or how people can make sense of the drudgery of work, or how they make sense of bodily affliction or social discrimination. Had he considered these he might have found a more comfortable place for secular ideology within culture and he might also have developed a less sanguine view of the capacity of religion to meet the functional requisite.

[5] O'Neill (1988: 493) is probably the leading interpreter to suggest that Bell's argument is clearly Durkheimian. He writes that postmodernism, 'inspires a Durkheimian

reflection on the ultimate value of the social bond which is backward-looking in Bell's neo-conservatism'.

[6] A sanitized and saccharin expression of the Western version of American small-town values can be inspected in a mawkish TV 'drama' made in the 1970s called 'The Little House on the Prairie' or in an earlier example called 'The Waltons'. The former is sufficiently appealing to be frequently rerun. Bell's claim runs counter to another set of myths, depicted in the traditional Western and gangster genres, in which coercion is the predominant means of social control.

[7] It needs to be stressed that the value-system has not disappeared. It re-emerged in the shape of the New Christian Right which was influential in shaping the moral tone of the Reagan–Bush Presidencies. In the 1980s and 1990s it takes the form of the 'Right to Life' movement which, like Temperance, seeks to use legal, coercive and even vigilante methods of social control.

[8] C.f., two much more recent analyses in the 'detraditionalization' school: Beck's discussion (1990) of individualization that explicitly uses the phrase 'I am I'; and Giddens' discussion (1991) of the relationship between reflexivity and identity.

[9] Bell encountered Horkheimer and Adorno at Columbia University.

[10] Bell distinguishes modernism from modernity in the following way: 'I think of modernity as a world outlook whose emphasis on life and thought is on experience, rather than tradition, as the touchstone of judgement. Modernism is a current in culture which expresses that outlook in symbolic and expressive terms' ('Afterword' to Campus-Verlag edition of CCC [in English ms.] 1990c: 7n; original italics).

[11] For Bell's detailed scholarship on Norman O. Brown and Michel Foucault see WP: 275–302.

8 REVELATIONS OF A TECHNOLOGIZED FUTURE

[1] Bell still had this project in mind when I interviewed him in November 1994. He also retrieved from his legendary basement two unpublished, book-length manuscripts and made them available to me. One is a history of socialism that began as a project for the *International Encyclopedia of the*

Social Sciences. The second is entitled 'The Exhausted Isle? Reflections on England in the 1970's'.

[2] For a discussion of Bell's location in the networks of social forecasting and futurology see Mullins (1973: 155–82). Mullins locates Bell as the central figure in these networks, participating in common projects with members of all the major forecasting groups (1973: 168).

[3] Bell is not always right about his predictive guesses but sometimes his prescience is breathtaking. We have only now come to accept the realistic possibility of an 'information superhighway' but Bell described it accurately in print in the mid-1960s: 'We will probably see a national information-computer-utility system, with tens of thousands of terminals in homes and offices "hooked" into giant central computers providing library and information services, retail ordering and billing services, and the like' (TY2000: 4). Perhaps the only correctives we might want to apply might be that the network is likely to be global rather than national and that the computers will only be gigantic in the sense that they will be informatically powerful rather than physically large. Fortunately, his prediction about (intentional) climatic modification appears to be a little way off.

[4] Bell estimates that this last one is, 'perhaps the most important and certainly the most refractory to prediction' (TY2000: 6).

[5] The forecasting methodology employed by the intellectuals that formed The Commission on the Year 2000 did not closely follow Bell's prescriptions. They divided their activities into two parts: a first group explored a series of 'alternative worlds', projecting trend lines under varying assumptions and estimating likely configurations; while a second worked on the methodological difficulties of forecasting. It would probably be fair to say that after ten years they had failed to produce a coherent forecast for the year 2000. Certainly, they published nothing like the Club of Rome report (Meadows *et al.* 1976) that Bell frequently criticizes for its predictive inadequacy (see e.g. 1987: 17).

[6] It is not always accepted that such an outcome is inevitable – the electronic anarchy of the Internet and the capacity of individual hackers to wreak chaos in computer networks suggest an entirely different possibility to that suggested by Bell.

[7] Bell elsewhere recognizes the contributions made by these political decisions. See e.g. DHB: 65–6. Curiously, his general explanations of inflation and other macro-economic problems fail to mention political agency, much less ideology. But then ideology had, of course, come to an end.

9 DAZZLING THE GOYIM

[1] As it happens, I thought I did – but modesty would not allow a self-portrait.
[2] Bell regards Wald's book as 'cock-eyed' (Bell to Waters 30/8/93).
[3] Some of what follows is drawn from Turner's excellent essay (1989).
[4] In an opposing view O'Neill (1988) finds clear parallels between Bell and Jameson.
[5] As Steinfels (1979: 186) indicates, Bell's style certainly places him alongside the classics, 'his style is itself a reproach to modern hedonism, an amassment and mobilization of data reminiscent of the great figures of Victorian social science'.

References

Students and scholars wishing to introduce themselves directly to the work of Daniel Bell can usefully do so by reading three items: the epilogue to EI; the foreword to the 1977 paperback edition of COPIS; and the foreword to the 1978 edition of CCC. These summarize the three big ideas but it would be better to read the whole of COPIS and CCC. The best short secondary sources are the chapters by Steinfels and Turner. The best full-length study is probably the one by Leibowitz.

BOOKS AND MONOGRAPHS WRITTEN OR EDITED BY DANIEL BELL

These are listed alphabetically by the reference abbreviation used in the text. The editions listed are the ones cited in the text. Details of other editions are given in parentheses.

(CCC) *The Cultural Contradictions of Capitalism*, 2nd edn with new foreword, London: Heinemann, 1979 [1st edn, New York: Basic, 1976].

(CET) (ed. with I. Kristol) *The Crisis in Economic Theory*, New York: Basic, 1981.

(COPIS) *The Coming of Post-Industrial Society: A Venture in Social Forecasting*, pbk edn with new foreword. New York:

Basic (Harper Torchbook), 1976 [1st edn, New York: Basic, 1975; 1st British edn, London: Heinemann, 1974].

(CSRU) (ed. with I. Kristol) *Confrontation: the Student Revolt and the Universities*, New York: Basic, 1969.

(CT) (ed. with I. Kristol) *Capitalism Today*, New York: New American Library, 1971 [1st edn New York: Basic, 1970].

(DHB) (with L. Thurow) *The Deficits: How Big? How Long? How Dangerous?*, New York: NYUP, 1985.

(EI) *The End of Ideology: On the Exhaustion of Political Ideas in the Fifties*, with new afterword (reprint of pbk edn). Cambridge: Harvard University Press, 1988 [1st edn Glencoe: Free Press, 1960; 1st Free Press pbk edn 1965].

(MS) *Marxian Socialism in the United States*, Princeton: Princeton University Press, 1967 [originally published in D. Egbert and S. Persons (eds) *Socialism and American Life* (Princeton Studies in American Civilization, Number 4), Princeton: Princeton University Press, 1952].

(RGE) *The Reforming of General Education: The Columbia College Experience in its National Setting*, New York: Columbia University Press, 1966

(RR) (ed.) *The Radical Right: The New American Right expanded and updated*, Garden City: Anchor, 1964 [1st edn as *The New American Right*, New York: Criterion, 1955; RR 1st published Garden City: Doubleday, 1963].

(SS) *The Social Sciences since the Second World War (Issues in Contemporary Civilization)*, New Brunswick: Transaction, 1982 [originally published in *The Great Ideas Today*, Chicago: Encyclopedia Britannica, 1979, 1980].

(TTR) *The Third Technological Revolution – and its Possible Socioeconomic Consequences*, Japan: Shukan Diamond, 1990.

(TY2000) (ed.) *Towards the Year 2000: Work in Progress*, Boston: Beacon, 1968 [originally published in *Daedalus* (Summer 1967)].

(WD) *Work and its Discontents*, New York: League for Industrial Democracy, 1970 [1st edn Boston: Beacon, 1956; subsequently expanded and republished in EI: 227–72].

(WP) *The Winding Passage: Sociological Essays and Journeys*, with a new foreword by I. Horowitz. New Brunswick: Transaction, 1991 [1st edn Boston: Abt, 1980].

ARTICLES BY DANIEL BELL

This list only includes items to which specific reference is made in the text. All but a few of Bell's academic articles are anthologized in his books.

(n.d.) 'Cultural Universals and a Universal Culture' (unpublished).

(n.d.) 'Marx and the Concept of Class' (unpublished).

(1947) 'Adjusting Men to Machines' *Commentary* (Jan): 79–88.

(1964) 'Twelve Modes of Prediction' *Daedalus* 93(3): 845–80.

(1965a) 'The Disjunction between Culture and Social Structure' *Daedalus* 94(1): 208–22.

(1965b) 'The Study of the Future' *The Public Interest* (1: summer): 119–30.

(1967a) 'The Post-Industrial Society: A Speculative View' in E. Hutchings and E. Hutchings (eds) *Scientific Progress and Human Values*, New York: Elsevier.

(1967b) 'Notes on the Post-Industrial Society (I)' *The Public Interest* (6 Winter): 24–35.

(1967c) 'Notes on the Post-Industrial Society (II)' *The Public Interest* (7 Spring): 102–18.

(1970) 'Quo Warranto? – Notes on the Governance of the Universities in the 1970's' *The Public Interest* (19 Spring): 53–68.

(1971a) 'The Post-Industrial Society: The Evolution of an Idea' *Survey* 16(1): 102–68.

(1971b) 'Religion in the Sixties' *Social Research* 38(3): 447–97.

(1971) with F. Bourricaud, J. Floud, G. Sartori, K. Tominaga and P. Wiles) 'The Post-Industrial Society – A Symposium' *Survey* 16(1): 1–77.

(1978) 'Social Forecasting – A Matrix: 1978–2000' (unpublished).

(1979) 'The Social Framework of the Information Society' in M. Dertouzos and J. Moses (eds) *The Computer Age*, Cambridge: MITP, 163–211.

(1981) 'First Love and Early Sorrows' *Partisan Review* 48(4): 532–51.

(1987) 'The World and the United States in 2013' *Daedalus* 116(3): 1–31.

(1989) 'American Exceptionalism Revisited: The Role of Civil Society' *The Public Interest* 95(Spring): 38–56.

(1990a) 'Resolving the Contradictions of Modernity and Modernism' *Society* 27(3; 4): 43–50; 66–75.

(1990b) 'The Misreading of Ideology: The Social Determination of Ideas in Marx's Work' *Berkeley Journal of Sociology* 35: 1–54.

(1990c) 'Afterword' to the Campus-Verlag German edition of CCC (unpublished in English).

(1992) 'The Break-up of Space and Time: Technology and Society in a Post-Industrial Age' Pittsburgh: American Sociological Association annual meeting (unpublished).

(1993) 'Downfall of the Business Giants' *Dissent* (Summer): 316–23.

OTHER WORKS

Items that include substantial commentary on Bell's work are marked with an asterisk

Abercrombie, N., S. Hill and B. Turner (1980) *The Dominant Ideology Thesis*, London: Allen & Unwin.

Alexander, J. (1982) *Postivism, Presuppositions and Current Controversies (Theoretical Logic in Sociology Vol. 1)* London: Routledge.

*Archer, M. (1990) 'Theory, Culture and Post-industrial Society' in M. Featherstone (ed.) *Global Culture*, London: Sage: 207–36.

*Badham, R. (1984) 'The Sociology of Industrial and Post-industrial Societies' *Current Sociology* 32(1): 1–141.

Beck, U. (1992) *Risk Society*, London: Sage.

Block, F. (1990) *Postindustrial Possibilities*, Berkeley: California University Press.

*Bloom, A. (1986) *Prodigal Sons: The New York Intellectuals and their World*, New York: Oxford University Press.

Bourdieu, P. (1984) *Distinction*, London: Routledge.

Braverman, H. (1974) *Labor and Monopoly Capital*, New York: Monthly Review.

*Brick, H. (1986) *Daniel Bell and the Decline of Intellectual Radicalism*, Madison: Wisconsin University Press.

*Chernow, R. (1979) 'The Cultural Contradictions of Daniel Bell' *Change* 11(2): 12–17.

Clark, C. (1957) *The Conditions of Economic Progress*, London: Macmillan.

*Collins, R. (1981) 'Postindustrialism and Technocracy' in his *Sociology at Midcentury*, New York: Academic: 305–8.

Cooney, T. (1986) *The Rise of the New York Intellectuals: Partisan Review and its Circle*, Madison: Wisconsin University Press.

Crook, S., J. Pakulski and M. Waters (1992) *Postmodernization*, London: Sage.

Dahrendorf, R. (1959) *Class and Class Conflict in Industrial Society*, Stanford: Stanford University Press.

*Dittberner, J. (1979) *The End of Ideology and American Social Thought: 1930–1960*, Ann Arbor: UMI Research Press.

Featherstone, M. (ed.) (1990) *Global Culture*, London: Sage.

Foote, N. and P. Hatt (1953) 'Social Mobility and Economic Advancement' *American Economic Review* 18(2): 364–78.

Foucault, M. (1979) *Discipline and Punish*, New York: Vintage.

Foucault, M. (1981) *The History of Sexuality Vol. 1*, Harmondsworth: Penguin.

Frankel, B. (1987) *The Post-industrial Utopians*, Cambridge: Polity.

Giddens, A. (1985) *The Nation-state and Violence*, Cambridge: Polity.

Giddens, A. (1991) *Modernity and Self-identity*, Cambridge: Polity.

Habermas, J. (1972) *Knowledge and Human Interests*, London: Heinemann.

Habermas, J. (1981) 'Modernity versus Postmodernity' *New German Critique* 22 (Winter): 3–14.

*Habermas, J. (1983) 'Neoconservative Culture Criticism in the United States and West Germany' *Telos* (56): 75–89.

Habermas, J. (1984) *Reason and the Rationalization of Society (The Theory of Communicative Action Vol. 1)*, Boston: Beacon.

Habermas, J. (1987) *The Critique of Functionalist Reason (The Theory of Communicative Action Vol. 2)*, Cambridge: Polity.

Habermas, J. (1992) *The Structural Transformation of the Public Sphere*, Cambridge: Polity.

*Hagan, R. (1975) 'Societal Disjunction and Axial Theory: Review Commentary on the Social Theory of Daniel Bell' *Review of Social Theory* 3(2): 40–4.

Harvey, D. (1988) *The Condition of Postmodernity*, Oxford: Blackwell.

*Hill, R. (1974) 'The Coming of Post-industrial Society' *The Insurgent Sociologist* 4(3): 37–51.

Holmwood, J., and A. Stewart (1991) *Explanation and Social Theory*, Basingstoke: Macmillan.

Holton, G. (1962) 'Scientific Research and Scholarship: Notes Towards the Design of Proper Scales' *Daedalus* 91(2): 362–99.

Howe, I. (1982) 'The Range of the New York Intellectual' in B. Rosenberg and E. Goldstein (eds) *Creators and Disturbers*, New York: Columbia University Press.

Inglehart, R. (1990) *Culture Shift in Advanced Industrial Society*, Princeton: Princeton University Press.

Jameson, F. (1984) 'Postmodernism: Or the Cultural Logic of Late Capitalism' *New Left Review* (146): 53–92.

*Jumonville, N. (1991) *Critical Crossings: The New York Intellectuals in Postwar America*, Berkeley: California University Press.

Kadushin, C. (1974) *The American Intellectual Elite*, Boston: Little Brown.

Kern, H. and M. Schumann (1984) *Das Ende der Arbeitsteilung?*, Munich: Beck.

*Kivisto, P. (1981) 'The Theorist as Seer: The Case of Bell's Postindustrial Society' *Quarterly Journal of Ideology* 5(2): 39–43.

*Kleinberg, B. (1973) *American Society in the Postindustrial Age*, Columbus: Merrill.

Kuhns, W. (1971) *The Post-industrial Prophets*, New York: Harper.

*Kumar, K. (1978) *Prophecy and Progress: The Sociology of Industrial and Post-industrial Society*, Harmondsworth: Penguin.

Lasch, C. (1972) 'Toward a Theory of Post-industrial Society' in M. Hancock and G. Sjoberg (eds) *Politics in the Post-Welfare State*, New York: Columbia University Press, 36–50.

Lash, S., and J. Urry (1987) *The End of Organised Capitalism*, Cambridge: Polity.

Lash, S., and J. Urry (1994) *Economies of Signs and Space*, London: Sage.

Laslett, J. and S. Lipset (1974) *Failure of a Dream? Essays in the History of American Socialism*, Garden City: Anchor.

*Leibowitz, N. (1985) *Daniel Bell and the Agony of Modern Liberalism*, Westport: Greenwood.

*Longstaff, S. (1987) 'Daniel Bell and Political Reconciliation' *Queen's Quarterly* 94(3): 660–5.

Lukács, G. (1968) *History and Class Consciousness*, London: Merlin.

Lyotard, J. (1984) *The Postmodern Condition*, Manchester: Manchester University Press.

McLuhan, M. (1964) *Understanding Media*, London: Routledge.

Malinowski, B. (1939) 'The Group and the Individual in Functional Analysis' *American Journal of Sociology* 44: 938–64.

Mandeville, B. ([1714] 1924) *The Fable of the Bees*, Oxford: Clarendon.

*Marien, M. (1973) 'Daniel Bell and the End of Normal Science' *The Futurist* 7(5): 262–8.

Meadows, D., D. Meadows, J. Randers and W. Behrens (1976) *The Limits to Growth*, Scarborough: Signet.

Miles, I., and J. Gershuny (1986) 'The Social Economics of Information Technology' in M. Ferguson (ed.) *New Communication Technologies and the Public Interest*, London: Sage.

*Miller, S. (1975) 'Notes on Neo-Capitalism' *Theory and Society* 2(1): 1–35.

Mullins, N. (1973) *Theories and Theory Groups in Contemporary American Sociology*, New York: Harper & Row.

*Nichols, T. (1975) Review of COPIS *Sociology* 9: 349–52.

Offe, C. (1984) *Contradictions of the Welfare State*, London: Hutchinson.

*O'Neill, J. (1988) 'Religion and Postmodernism: The Durkheimian Bond in Bell and Jameson' *Theory Culture and Society* 5(2–3): 493–508.

*Pahl, R. (1975) Review of COPIS *Sociology* 9: 347–9.

Piore, M. and C. Sabel (1984) *The Second Industrial Divide*, New York: Basic.

*Rejai, M. (ed.) (1971) *Decline of Ideology?*, Chicago: Aldine.

Robertson, R. (1992) *Globalization*, London: Sage.

*Rose, M. (1991) *The Post-modern and the Post-industrial*, Cambridge: Cambridge University Press.

*Ross, G. (1974) 'The Second Coming of Daniel Bell' in R. Miliband and J. Saville (eds) *The Socialist Register 1974*, London: Merlin: 331–48.

*Rule, J. (1971) 'The Problem with Social Problems' *Politics and Society* 1 (Fall): 47–56.

Schumpeter, J. (1942) *Capitalism, Socialism and Democracy*, New York: Harper.

*Simons, H. (1988) *Jewish Times*, Boston: Houghton Mifflin.

*Stearns, P. (1973) 'Is there a Post-industrial Society?' *Society* 11(1): 11–25.

*Steinfels, P. (1979) *The NeoConservatives*, New York: Simon & Schuster.

*Tilman, R. and J. Simich (1984) 'On the Use and Abuse of Thorstein Veblen in Modern American Sociology, II: Daniel Bell and the "Utopianizing" of Veblen's Contribution and Its

Integration by Robert Merton and C. W. Mills' *American Journal of Economics and Sociology* 43(10): 103–28.

Touraine, A. (1971) *The Post-industrial Society*, New York: Random House.

Touraine, A. (1977) 'Crisis or Transformation?' in N. Birnbaum (ed.) *Beyond the Crisis*, New York: Oxford University Press: 17–49.

*Turner, B. (1989) 'From Postindustrial Society to Postmodern Politics: – the Political Sociology of Daniel Bell' in J. Gibbins (ed.) *Contemporary Political Culture*, London: Sage: 199–217.

Vico, G. ([1744] 1984) *The New Science of Giambattista Vico*, Ithaca: Cornell University Press.

*von der Ohe, W., T. Drabek, R. Hall, R. Hill, J. Lopreato, P. Marcus and M. Phillips with a reply by D. Bell (1973) 'The Coming of Post-Industrial Society: A Review Symposium' *Summation* 3(2):60–103.

Wald, A. (1987) *The New York Intellectuals*, Chapel Hill: UNCP.

Waters, M (1994) 'Succession in the Stratification System' *International Sociology* 9(3): 295–312.

Waters, M. (1995) *Globalization*, London: Routledge.

*Waxman, C. (ed.) (1968) *The End of Ideology Debate*, New York: Simon & Schuster (Clarion).

Wright, E. (1985) *Classes*, London: Verso.

Index

UNIVERSITY OF WOLVERHAMPTON
LIBRARY